To Renee — my dear "homesteader" & "antiques" Love in Christ, Diane Christmas 1987

THE HOMESTEAD COOKBOOK

THE HOMESTEAD COOKBOOK

Edited by Virginia Paul
For Home and Family Use

Lora Denny making soap in the yard at the John W. Denny home, Seattle in 1906. *Courtesy of the Seattle Historical Society*

SUPERIOR PUBLISHING COMPANY
SEATTLE

Copyright 1976 by Superior Publishing Company
Seattle, Washington

All Rights Reserved

Library of Congress Cataloging in Publication Data

Paul, Virginia
The homestead cookbook.

1. Cookery, Americana.   I. Title.
TX715.P328   641.5'973   76-16158
ISBN 0-87564-340-X

First Edition

Printed and Bound in the United States of America

TABLE OF CONTENTS

FOREWORD 6
MEATS 11
    Beef 11
    Lamb and Mutton 20
    Fish 22
    Game/Fowl 24
    Game/Venison 27
    Soups 28
MISCELLANEOUS, RECEIPTS 33
BREADS AND CEREALS 34
BEVERAGES 41
BUTTER, CHEESE and EGGS 45
SWEETS 48
VEGETABLES 57
JELLIES and PRESERVES 65
SUNDRYING, FERMENTATION - PICKLING, VINEGAR 78
HERBS, PLANTS, ROOTS and REMEDIES 85
    Remedies 85
REMINDERS 86
MISCELLANEOUS 100
    Measures, Tables and Weights 113
    Omens 114
    Water Witching 115
ACKNOWLEDGEMENTS 117
MEMORABILIA 118-119-120-121-122
INDEX 123-124-125-126-127

FOREWORD

The Homestead days are gone. The early 1900s brought an end to a spectacular era in American History. There is no more land available for homesteading under the original law.

The Homestead Law was an agricultural reform law signed on May 20th 1862 by Abraham Lincoln. It was not perfect but it gave to heads of families or persons over 21 years of age 160 acres of public land with the requirement that they would improve the land and live on it for five years. Most of the land available for homesteading was in the West. This land was largely desert or semi-arid land too marginal to support a family on the acreage allotment.

The most expansive population movement in America occurred during the period covered by this book. Settlers in the Western States and Territories increased by hundreds of thousands and the Mid-west by more than one million immigrants from Europe and the East. During this ingression, settlement fairly leaped from the Eastern United States to the Pacific Coast to be followed in thirty years by the occupation of the intervening territory, the 'Great American Desert.'

This area, though not a desert in fact, was entirely different than the forested, moisture-laden frontiers to which American pioneers had been accustomed. Adjustments were required in the basic tactics of survival and of crop raising.

Life's most difficult challenge was the provision of food, clothing and shelter for the family, the methods of which had changed little from the time of the Revolutionary War period. People ate the same basic foods, plentiful in season, with variations based on the products that could be grown in the area.

To this new land, they brought with them their traditional eating habits, adapting their customary dishes to the natural resources of the area—the Indian foods, the game and birds of the plains and timberlands, the trout and fish from the rivers and ocean.

Added to wild game, were domesticated animals and poultry as farm flocks and herds multiplied.

The basic diet was composed of food grains, meats, animal fats, sugar, potatoes and legumes. Of their garden and field crops, many originated with the American Indians—corn, beans, cotton, Irish and sweet potatoes, tomatoes, pumpkins, squashes and sunflowers. Corn was a crop that pioneers depended upon for their rudimentary food grain supply.

Courtesy of the Seattle Historical Society

Many early settlers brought with them seedlings of fruit trees, slips of shrubs, flower and garden seeds. Aromatic flowers, house-plants and shrubs were used for flavoring in cooking and preserving. The planting of orchards and vegetables was among the first chores to be undertaken.

Drying, storing and preserving of foods took some of the monotony out of meals through winter months. Methods of preservation used at the time go back thousands of years in history. Meat was probably preserved by accident as it dried and smoked over Stoneage fires. Fermentation has been used for centuries to produce beverages. Certain food have been kept by pickling. From the earliest of times, salt has been employed as a preservative.

With the coming of Spring dandelion, polk, lamb's quarters, dock, mustard, pigweed, ferns, Russian thistle, meadow cowslips and snow thistles were eagerly sought in the clearings and meadows to supplement the daily menu. Pioneer homemakers prepared them, not only as a welcome addition to the diet, but as tonics to purify the blood. It was not known that these plants contained Vitamin A and C which made vital contributions to the physical well being of homestead families.

Preventative medicine was yet to come. A doctor was often miles away and only under the most dire and acute circumstances was he called. Household remedies were relied upon to ease the distress of common ailments and less severe injury. Some of the plants and herbs used in preparing old-fashioned remedies have been found to possess medicinal properties.

In coping with the problems of homestead life, ingenuity and practical know-how were exercised to the utmost. The rule was 'make it do or do without.'

Those were the times when a man's word was his bond; when the spirit of friendship and helpfulness—neighbor to neighbor—rose to its greatest height; when hospitality was at its peak; when opportunities to get together were cherished—be it a barn raising, community picnic, dance or church service.

The stalwart, determined faces pictured in this book reveal most eloquently the cost of survival and the grim determination to succeed. These peo-

Emigrants crossing the plains in 1869. People traveling by wagon train to the western frontier faced adversities of every nature. The mother of a two-year old baby, in recalling the trials of the trail, said they were chased by Indians, lost all of their belongings and traveled by foot over hot desert sands. *Courtesy of the Seattle Historical Society*

ple of all backgrounds and heritages perpetuated the American Dream.

Chris Jouflas of Colorado spoke for many Americans when he told me, "With my roots in the Old World and my home in the New, I have the best of two worlds."

What would we be without them?

The purpose of this book is to record the ways in which sturdy, enterprising pioneers met the realities of self-preservation. The recipes, remedies and reminders are authentic. The old-fashioned remedies should never be used as substitutes for a doctor's advice or prescribed medications. The reader will notice variations in spelling, measurements and style which reflect the changes from more primitive methods to modern standards.

The material can be utilized and adapted to today's lifestyle. Many recipes can be used as written to broaden eating and living experiences, however, the greatest care should be exercised in the preparation and use of household items and remedies which may contain caustics or ingredients harmful to health.

I think the majority of Americans long for a return to the 'simple' life of yesteryear and the rewards of being self-sufficient. Whether or not these 'recipes for living' are tried, I hope "Homestead Cookery," provides many hours of family enjoyment.

Before starting on their journey, women and girls sewed all winter long making tents, wagon covers and clothing by hand. Some women cooked for as many as twenty men on an open fire baking bread, cakes and pies as well as more staple fare. Often as the end of the journey, there was only bread, bacon and sorghum left to eat. *Courtesy of the Seattle Historical Society*

now entitled to receive when the same quality of land is entered with money, one half to be paid by the person making the application at the time of so doing, and the other half on the issue of the certificate by the person to whom it may be issued, but this shall not be construed to enlarge the maximum of compensation now prescribed by law for any register or receiver: Provided, that nothing contained in this act shall be so construed as to impair or interfere in any manner whatever with existing preemption rights: And Provided, further, That all persons who may have filed their applications for a preemption right prior to the passage of this act shall be entitled to all privileges of this act: Provided, further, That no person who has served, or may hereafter serve, for a period of not less than fourteen days in the army or navy of the United States, either regular or volunteer, under the laws thereof, during the existence of an actual war, domestic or foreign, shall be deprived of the benefit of this act on account of not having attained the age of twenty-one years.

Sec. 7. And be it further enacted, That the fifth section of the act entitled "An act in addition to an act more effectually to provide for the punishment of certain crimes against the United States and for other purposes," approved the third of March, in the year eighteen hundred and fifty-seven, shall extend to all oaths, affirmations, and affidavits, required or authorized by this act.

Sec. 8. And be it further enacted, That nothing in this act shall be so construed as to prevent any person who has availed him or herself of the benefits of the first section of this act from paying the minimum price, or the price to which the same may have graduated, for the quantity of land so entered at any time before the expiration of the five years, and obtaining a patent therefor from the government, as in other cases provided by law, on making proof of settlement and cultivation as provided by existing laws granting preemption rights.

Galusha A. Grow
Speaker of the House of Representatives

Solomon Foot,
President of the Senate, pro tempore

Abraham Lincoln

Approved, May 20. 1862.

The closing portion of the Homestead Act approved on May 20, 1862. *Courtesy of the National Archives, Record Group photo Number 11.*

Courtesy of the National Archives, Photo #11-RB-5560 U.S. Signal Corps.

MEATS

Beef

Beef Barbecue in a Pit

Dig hole about 3 feet deep. Keep a good fire going for at least 4 hours so there is a deep bed of coals. Have beef cut in about 8 to 12 pound roasts. Season as you wish and put onions around it. Wrap in heavy paper and then several layers of burlap. When fire is ready dip wrapped meat packages in water and lay on top of coals. Cover immediately with dirt. (Burlap may char slightly but will not burn.)

Barbecue

Dig open pit 12 feet long and 3½ feet deep. Line pit with rocks and build hot fire. Heat for several hours and remove fire.

Steal a good cow beef, cut up in chunks and place chunks in strong, heavy cotton sacks. Use 1 pound for each outlaw to be served. Salt and pepper meat to taste.

Place heavy layer of wet straw over hot rocks. Keep straw wet until pit is covered so it will not catch fire. Place sacks of meat on wet straw. Cover meat with another heavy layer of wet straw. Cover this with more hot rocks. Cover the whole thing with 2½ or 3 feet of dirt. Watch for several hours because of fire hazard. Leave for 16 to 18 hours and open.

Boiled Beef Neck

Cut a whole neck in half and put on to boil using a little salt and cover the meat with cold water. Boil until tender when pierced with a fork. Add water from time to time to keep liquid about the same. When done remove from the broth and cool. This is grand to slice and use cold for a cold plate supper, or grind any amount you wish for sandwiches, seasoning with salt and pepper and part of the broth in which the beef was cooked. Serve hot between fresh buns.

The neck is very good for making mince meat.

The ground meat combined with cold boiled potatoes, seasoned and baked, makes a delicious hash for breakfast, dinner or supper.

Boiled Dinner

Take 6 pounds of corned beef brisket, 1 cabbage, 3 white turnips, 4 carrots, 6 potatoes, 6 beets, if available, and vinegar. Put the meat into a pot over a brisk fire with enough cold water to cover it and add 1 teaspoon of vinegar to each quart of water. Bring to a boil, remove the scum, reduce the heat to simmer until tender from three to four hours. About 45 minutes before it is to be served, skim off the fat and a portion of the liquid and put into another kettle. Put into this the cabbage and other vegetables and boil until tender.

Brown Ragout

Brown Ragout calls for cut up meat, whether boned or not into neat pieces about 2 inches long. Chuck, rump, shank, any of these cuts will produce a fine ragout.

Brown them over a good heat in a saute pan in several tablespoons of fat or drippings. Season with salt, pepper and a pinch of sugar. The addition of sugar gives the preparation a good, natural color. As soon as the pieces of meat are browned, pour off ¾ of the fat, sprinkle with flour and let it color a little, shaking the pot over the heat. Stir in water, stock or meat juice and put in a little crushed garlic and tomato sauce. Cook covered in the oven or on a very low heat for 45 minutes to an hour. Drain the pieces of meat, trim the fat, put them in another pot or in the same pot in which they were cooked, cover them with specific vegetables of your choice and pour over the sauce, strained and with the fat removed. Cook covered, simmering very gently for 45 minutes or an hour, or until the meat is tender, according to the kind of meat being used. Cooking in the oven is best. Serve in a deep dish or plate, placing the pieces of meat below and the vegetables on top. Pour the hot sauce over all.

Though many buffalo were killed just for the sport of it, the animal was the cattle of the plains. Buffalo were so essential to the Indians that their life-style and religion were build around them. Settlers, too, 'ate considerable buffalo meat' in making the long journey from their taking-off points along the Missouri River to the Pacific Coast. *Courtesy of the Seattle Historical Society*

Brown Stock or Bouillon

2 pounds beef (¼ to ½ bone)
1¼ quarts cold water
4 to 6 peppercorns
2 cloves
1 bay leaf
1 teaspoon salt
1 blade mace
1 teaspoon sweet herbs
Sprig parsley
1 tablespoon, each, of carrot, onion, celery, turnip

A good stock can be made by using left-over meat scraps and bones instead of the beef specified, and by substituting any available vegetables, such as the outer leaves of lettuce, celery tops, etc., for those given. After the stock is made, left-over vegetables, cereals, hard-cooked eggs, small pieces of meat, etc., may be diced or chopped and served in the soup.

Consommé

1 pound lean beef
1 pound veal
1¼ quarts cold water or 1 pint cold water and 1 pint chicken stock
2 peppercorns
1 clove
½ teaspoon sweet herbs
Sprig parsley
1 tablespoon each, celery, carrot, onion
1 teaspoon salt

MUTTON OR LAMB STOCK OR BROTH—Use the same ingredients as for brown stock or bouillon, using mutton or lamb instead of beef, and removing most of the fat from the meat.

Quick-Made Stock

Take 2 glasses or 10 ounces of water, 4 ounces of beef, some carrots, parsnips, onions, celery, in all about an ounce, and if you wish to add an aromatic, 1/3 of clove and a piece of garlic the size of a lentil. Chop the meat, as the greatest division of substance yields maximum of their nutritive elements, soften the vegetables on red hot ashes, or moisten and cook slightly in their own juices, this way they have more taste and yield their sweet juices more easily. Cut them into thin, round slices. To divide the clove, it is put between two sheets of paper and crushed with a blunt instrument. Treated this way it rapidly communicates its fragrance to the stock. If garlic is added, it should be scraped with a knife. Put everything into a sauce pan. Add water and salt and stir with a spoon and cover with a lid. Six minutes is enough to bring it to a boil. It will be difficult to remove the scum, so leave it. Once the stock pot has been heated to boiling, the smallest flame will be enough to keep it simmering and it requires no attention at all. You can forget about it completely for a half hour, although it would do no harm to leave it a little longer. After half an hour, it can be considered ready. The stock should be strained through a silk strainer.

Campfire Meal

Cut around 2 pounds of round of beef into cubes of one inch and put a cupful of chopped meat into a skillet. When the fat is rendered, remove the cracklings; throw the meat into the hot fat and shake over a hot fire until thoroughly brown. Add 2 rounded tablespoons of flour mixed with water to a quart of stock and stir until it boils. Add one saltspoon of pepper, a hunk of onion, and put the cover on the pot and cook slowly for an hour and a half.

Beef Brisket With Sauerkraut

4 pounds beef brisket	1 cup vinegar
Hot water	3 tablespoons brown sugar
1 tablespoon salt, pepper	1 uncooked potato, grated
	2 tablespoons grated onion
1 quart sauerkraut	

Cover brisket with water, season and simmer 1 to 1½ hours. Add sauerkraut, vinegar, onions, and brown sugar. Cook about 1 hour longer for meat to become tender. Add the potato and cook 10 minutes longer. This will serve eight.

Chili Con Carne

¼ cup olive oil	2 cloves garlic
2 pounds lean beef (cut in ¾ inch cubes)	1 tablespoon paprika
	2 teaspoons oregano
¼ pound beef suet (cut in ¾ inch cubes)	Salt and Pepper
	1 cup minced onions

Heat the olive oil, add the meat and suet and cook until meat is brown. Add onions and garlic and cook about 5 minutes, stirring constantly; then stir in the chili powder, paprika, oregano, salt and pepper. Add 1 cup water and simmer until meat is tender. Add more water if necessary.

WITH BEANS—Serve chili with baked beans, rice or Lima beans; or add 4 cups red kidney beans to the meat before simmering.

Crusty Beef Roll

1 cup chopped onion	⅓ cup milk
½ cup chopped green pepper	Roll Mixture:
	¾ cup milk
¾ pound ground beef	2 cups packaged or homemade biscuit mix
½ cup fine, dry bread crumbs	
1 teaspoon salt	Tomato sauce
Pepper	

Cook onion and green pepper in hot fat until soft. Add ground beef; brown slightly. Add bread crumbs, salt, pepper and ⅓ cup milk; mix thoroughly. Add ¾ cup milk to biscuit mix; mix well. Roll to ½ inch thickness. Spread with the cooked meat mixture. Roll, seal ends. Cook in 400 oven about 40 minutes. Serve with tomato sauces. Serves 6 generously.

Curing Meat by Salting

Cleanse the meat in salted water and weigh. An amount of salt equal to 1/10th the weight of the meat and an amount of saltpetre equal to 1/40th of the weight of salt is measured out. Mix the salt thoroughly. Dry seived salt is used, divided into three parts and to each part add ⅓ of the saltpetre which has been crushed and seived. One of the piles is rubbed into the meat, one is spinkled over it and the last is saved for sprinkling when the meat is rebedded. Break the salt pack after 5 days, remove discolored salt and rebed the meat with the remaining salt. The meat can be kept by this manner for a long time. When the meat is to be used, wash off the excess salt and soak overnight. Prepare as desired. The meat can be dried and smoked.

Dried Beef

Brown salt like coffee and while hot roll each piece of beef in it thoroughly; pack in a crock and let it remain five days; take out, wash well and hang up to dry.

Dried Beef

For 20 pounds beef—

Mix 1 pint salt, 1 teaspoon saltpeter and ¼ pound brown sugar. Divide into three parts. Rub into meat for three successive days. Turn beef in the juice formed for 1 week, once each day. Hang in a dry cooler place to dry until finished. Put a little extra salt in the holes cut for the cord to hang by. Chunks of beef could be from five to ten pounds in weight. If you like a smoked flavor, smoke the meat after it has quit dripping, then dry. Slice thin when serving.

Beef, Dried, Fricasseed

Melt 1 tablespoonful of butter, with ½ pint of milk, or cream sauce; add 1 cup of beef chopped fine (that has been soaked in boiling water for 15 minutes) and 2 beaten eggs and stir until the sauce is thick. Serve on toast.

Empanaditas De Carne

1 pound boiling meat	1 teaspoon salt
1½ cup raisins	1 cake yeast
2 cups applesauce or jam	1½ cup water or milk
	3 tablespoon fat
1 cup sugar	1½ teaspoon salt
1 teaspoon coriander seed	2 tablespoons sugar
	4-5 cups sifted flour
½ teaspoon cinnamon	
½ cup shelled pinon nuts	(all-purpose)

Grind meat and add the next 8 ingredients making a paste. If paste is too dry add a little meat stock; paste should be moist. Head ½ cup of the liquid to lukewarm and add yeast. Add enough flour to make a medium dough. Roll out pastry ⅛ inch thick and about 4 inches in diameter. Place 1½ teaspoon meat paste on ½ of the pastry; fold the other half over and pinch edges together; then make a turn back in the dough by taking edges between thumb and forefinger, pressing together and turning back in ridges. Let turnovers stand for 5 minutes then deep fat fry.

Hamburg Steak

2 pounds chopped beef	Onion-juice
¼ pound suet	Flour
Butter	Salt and pepper

Have the butcher chop the beef and suet together twice. Press it into a flat steak about three-fourths of an inch thick, sprinkle with salt, pepper, a little onion-juice and flour. Broil on a fine wire broiler or sauté in a little fat. Spread with butter and serve on a hot dish. This steak is sometimes shaped into small, thin, flat cakes. When it is sautéed, a gravy may be made by thickening the juices in the pan, to which a little water has been added. Two tablespoons of melted butter and one tablespoon minced onion mixed with the meat and seasonings improves Hamburg steak.

Aspic Jelly

2 pounds beef	Salt and pepper
½ pound ham or bacon	1 egg-white
Sweet herbs	2 tablespoons lemon-juice

Put the beef into the pot and, if desired, veal or beef bones also, though they require longer boiling to dissolve the gelatin. Add the ham or bacon and all the sweet herbs, such as thyme, basil, parsley and marjoram, and salt and pepper to taste. Boil for three or four hours; strain and put away to cool. When cold, take off all the fat and sediment. Throw into it the slightly beaten egg-white, and the lemon-juice, place again on the fire, boil for a few minutes and strain through a jelly-bag.

This is used for molding cold meat.

Beef Jerky

When the Indians made jerky it was pulled or 'jerked' in strips from the buffalo, venison or beef carcass. You can either jerk or cut in strips up to one-half inch thick and string each strip on a string or wire. While you are stripping the meat, have a large pot of heavily salted water setting to boil. The density of salt to water should be about a quarter of a cup to a gallon of water. Dip the meat into the boiling brine just long enough for the meat to lose its red color. This takes but a few seconds. Let the water drip off for a few minutes; lay on a platter and salt and pepper generously. Hang the meat to dry in the sun. It will take three days to dry properly. Place in a sack and store in a cool place. It will keep for a long time.

Beef Juice

Take a pound of round steak with no fat on it, cut thick, broil slightly and press the juice out with a lemon squeezer or a meat press. You generally get from two to four ounces of juice from a pound of beef. This, seasoned with salt, may be given cold or it may be warmed by placing the cup which holds it into warm water. It should not be heated enough to coagulate the albumen which is in solution and which then appears as flakes of meat floating in the fluid.

Beef Juice

Broil a thick piece of steak 3 minutes. Squeeze all juice out with a lemon squeezer into a cup. Salt very lightly and give like beef tea.

Pasties

1 large raw potato	Parsley
¼ pound crumbled hamburger or cubed beef	Onion
	Salt
	Pepper
2 small turnips	

Roll out pie dough as for pie—about an 8 inch circle—on half of it place a layer of your potato shredded, a layer of meat, a layer of turnip, lots of chopped parsley, a little onion, salt and pepper.

Fold dough over and seal as you would a pie—slits on top. Place on a pan and bake in oven. After the first half hour add 2 or 3 tablespoons water through holes in top—cook another half hour or until done. One per person.

Pemmican

Pemmican was prepared by the Indians to tide them over periods of short food supply. It is a mixture of pulverized dried meat, usually buffalo, and wild berries. Pemmican is stored in the dry state. Indians carried it with them in a deer skin pouch called a PARFLICH. When they stopped along the trail they poured into the mixture hot fat which they had rendered from a strip of suet. To make Pemmican combine equal parts of pulverized dried beef, crushed berries and hot fat, put in a flat pan and cut into bars when cool.

Pickled Flank

Remove surplus fat and tough membrane from flank and roll tightly with grain of lean meat lengthwise, so it will be sliced crosswise of grain when cold. Tie or skewer the roll securely and boil tender in water to cover. Season to taste with salt, pepper and one-half (or more) cup vinegar. Cool in broth, slice and pack in suitable container and cover with hot broth, boiled down until it congeals when cold. Whole spices may be added if desired.

Pickle for Beef or Ham

For each hundred pounds of beef or ham use 9 pounds of salt, 4 ounces of saltpeter, 2 ounces of saleratus and 2 quarts of molasses; add water to make enough brine to cover meat. Scald brine. Skim and let cool before pouring on meat.

Pot Roast

Take 4 pounds of round and boil four hours, boiling down until there is no water left in the kettle and allow meat to brown. Pour in water, enough for gravy and thicken with flour, seasoned to suit.

Potted Beef

Cut up 3 pounds beef (round), into 5 or 6 pieces and put it in jar with ½ tumblerful cold water. Let it simmer for 5 hours. Then put through mincer and mix well 2 tablespoonfuls anchovy sauce, salt and pepper to taste, leaving out as much butter as will cover the top of the jars. (Recipe calls for ½ pound butter) Melt the butter and pour over.

Kansas Chili

1 pound ground beef	1 tablespoon chili relish
1 cup chili beans (dried)	2 cups tomato juice
1 tablespoon osago leaves	1 pepper pod (if desired)
	4 small onions, ground
1 tablespoon cumin seed	2 teaspoons salt

Soak beans overnight and cook with diced bacon until tender. Remove bacon. Brown beef and onions. Add tea made from steeping osago leaves and cumin seed for 10 minutes. Add tomato juice and cook until meat is tender. Simmer with beans and other seasonings until well seasoned.

Garanches

One cup cornmeal and 1 teaspoon salt cooked in boiling water to make a mush. Cool slightly. Keep the hands wet with cold water, shape 6 cases 3 inches in diameter and ⅜ inch thick. Bake on a well-greased griddle. Turn only once and do not get too brown. Split cases, scoop out insides and fill. For filling combine ¾ cup ground cooked beef (leftovers as roast are very acceptable), 2 tablespoons chopped onion and 6 tablespoons chili sauce. Season to taste with salt and pepper. Fill cases, place lids on, heat again on griddle and serve with Parmesan cheese.

Spitted Meat

To spit a hindquarter of meat, rub with a mixture of flour and pepper and hang in a cool place for three or four days. Trim and cover with flour and water paste, wrap in strong paper and tie. Roast on the spit, basting often, for three or four hours. A short time before removing from the spit, remove the paper and flour-paste coating and brown over a hot fire.

Wagoneer Stew

Take not less than 2 sage hens or six quail or jacksnipe, unjoint and place in a gallon of water with about a dozen squares of salt pork or beef and a liberal amount of pepper. Boil briskly for 45 minutes then add 2 onions and a half-dozen potatoes chopped fine and boil until the potatoes and onions are done; then add a few dumplings. When the dumplings begin to fall to pieces, the stew is ready to serve.

Tacos

1½ pounds ground beef	1 dozen tortillas
2 small, or 1 large tomato	Half head lettuce
	½ pound long horn cheese
2 small, or 1 large clove garlic	Hot sauce (taco sauce or Mexican hot sauce)
1 medium size onion	Salt to taste

Brown meat in skillet in small amount of fat. When brown, add tomato, garlic and onion, diced in very small pieces. Salt to taste. Let simmer 10 minutes. Add large spoonful of meat mixture to tortilla, fold in the middle, and brown in hot fat. Drain, add grated long horn cheese, and shredded lettuce. Last, add hot sauce if desired.

The little sod home of the prairie and the Southwest. The grass-covered surface soil held together by matted roots was cut into building blocks for the homesteaders in areas where logs, wood, mortar and stone were not available. The sod 'shanty' could be put up in a hurry and would often be erected over a dug-out in the side of a hill, the roof of which might be farmed along with the surrounding land of the homestead tract. *Courtesy of Jim Crosby*

Red Flannel Hash

4 medium beets, cooked
3 medium potatoes, cooked
2 cups chopped cooked beef
¼ teaspoon pepper
¼ cup butter
¼ cup chopped onion
½ cup cream
1 teaspoon salt

Chop beets and potatoes and mix with the chopped beef; season with salt and pepper. Melt butter in a heavy skillet; add onion and saute until golden brown. Add the meat mixture and pour cream over top. Cook slowly for about 15 to 20 minutes until brown crust has formed, or bake in moderate oven, for 35 minutes. Turn onto hot platter and serve at once.

This Red Flannel Hash is an excellent way to use up leftover meat or vegetables. Almost any combination of meat and vegetables may be used. Remember to season well. Serves 4 to 6.

Scarlet or Pickled Tongue

Simmer the tongue for two hours in salted water or until tender when pierced with a fork. Remove from the liquid and cool. The skin will remove easily. Trim away the fat and slice in ¼-inch slices. Combine 1 cup of vinegar, 1 cup of water and 1 cup of sugar. Put ½ teaspoon of cinnamon, ½ teaspoon of cloves and ½ teaspoon of allspice in a small, finely woven bag or wrap and tie in a piece of muslin.

Boil the sliced tongue in this pickling juice for about ten minutes. Put the tongue in a heat resistant glass jar, pour the hot pickling juice over it, drop in the spice bag and seal. The tongue will be ready in about five or six days.

Smoked Meats

There are usually no windows in a smokehouse. An outlet for smoke is made in the ceiling. Sides of beef or venison, especially the ribs and brisket are good cuts to use. Hog hams are probably the most widely used cuts for smoking. Birds and poultry can also be smoked. The meat is soaked in a pickling brine, thoroughly wiped dry and hung in the smokehouse away from the fire, not directly over it, to ensure that the meat be thoroughly penetrated. Smoking is a slow process and should be continued until the meat is impregnated to the degree of flavour desired. It is best accomplished at a heat of about 90 degrees which the experienced smoker can determine by holding his hand in the smokehouse. Hickory wood smoke imparts an excellent flavour and aroma to the meat.

Stew

Cut up steak in neat square pieces, stew in the usual way slowly, adding pepper and salt, a green apple sliced, a little curry and small spoonful jam. Serve hot, with border of boiled rice.

Stew With Bread Dumplings

Brown small pieces of beef in hot fat. Add chopped onion, salt and pepper and lots of paprika. Add enough water to cook meat and steam 1½ hours. Add bread dumplings and cook ½ hour longer.

BREAD DUMPLINGS:

Soak ½ loaf of bread in warm water and squeeze dry. Add 3 eggs, 3 tablespoons shortening and 3 tablespoons milk (4 tablespoons of cream may be substituted for fat and milk). Salt and pepper to taste. Add flour enough to make stiff dough. Drop into meat broth and cook as directed.

Pressed Beef

5 or 6 pound beef, thick flank, pickled; if the beef has been long in pickle, wash it, put into a pan of cold water, bring to the boil and skim; add a few sliced vegetables and simmer slowly about 2 hours. Lift out, remove bone, press with a weight on top. When quite cool wipe off grease and cover with glaze. Dish and garnish with aspic and parsley. The beef may be decorated with a little butter beaten till creamy and put into a forcing bag and tube.

Beef Tea

Take out the bone of a 2 pound hough, or shin of beef, remove the fat, and cut the meat into pieces about an inch square. Put these into a basin or jar, with a slight seasoning of pepper and salt, and a sprig or two of green parsley. Add ½ pint of cold water, cover closely, and put into a quick oven. May be put in about 6 or 7 in the evening, when there is a good fire, and allowed to remain all night. When cold in the morning, take off any fat and remove the meat. You need not strain the liquor, some of which may be just warmed up, not boiled, as required for use. The quantity of water will depend on the condition of the patient. If very weak, and only able to take a teaspoonful or so at a time, a ½ pint will be quite sufficient; if the tea is to be taken as a strengthening draught by a convalescent, twice that quantity, or even more, may be used.

The Borruff house on August 7, 1915. A family and all its possessions. *Courtesy of the Henderson Collection, Washington State University Library*

Tamale Pie

1½ pounds ground round
Salt and pepper
½ cup shortening
½ cup grated American cheese
1 chopped onion
2 tablespoons cornmeal
1 clove garlic
1 chopped sweet green pepper
1½ cup chopped fresh tomatoes
1 cup cornmeal
½ cup ripe olives (pitted)
3 cups boiling water
2 chili peppers cut fine
1 teaspoon salt
1 tablespoon chili powder

Cook onion, garlic and green pepper in hot fat until tender; add ground round and brown. Add tomatoes, ripe olives, chili peppers, salt and pepper and simmer 1 hour. Stir in grated cheese, 2 tablespoons cornmeal, chili powder and cook 5 minutes. Gradually add 1 cup cornmeal to 3 cups boiling salted water, stirring constantly until mixture thickens. Pour cornmeal mush over beef mixture. Bake at 400 degrees for 30 minutes and garnish with more ripe olives.

Short Ribs of Beef

Use a short rib of beef. Put into a saucepan with a slice of onion, a clove, a sliced carrot, a bunch of sweet herbs, salt and pepper (allow ¾ teaspoon salt and ⅛ tablespoon pepper to the pound of meat), ½ cup fruit juice and 4 cups water. Cover and cook slowly for two hours or more. Take up the meat, strain and skim the liquid, reduce half by rapid boiling, thicken with browned flour, pour over meat and serve with macaroni or noodles. Serves 5 or 6.

Calf's-Foot Jelly Stock

Divide and wash 4 calf's feet well and remove all fat, put into pan with 3 pints cold water, bring slowly to the boil, and skim well; simmer very slowly 6 hours, strain through wire sieve, allow to stand 12 hours; remove the fat, and it is ready for the jelly. It should be stiff enough to stand; if not, add a little isinglass.

Beef Tea by the Cold Method

Take a pound of finely chopped round steak, a coffee cup full of cold water and a pinch of salt. Place in a covered jar and set in a cold place for 5 or 6 hours or over night. It is well to shake occasionally. Strain and squeeze out all the juice by placing the meat in a coarse muslin cloth and twisting very hard. This beef juice is very nutritious and better than the extracts of beef which are sold in the stores.

Calf's-Foot Jelly

Put 1 quart calf's-foot stock, rind and juice of 3 lemons, 2 inches cinnamon stick, 2 cloves, and 6 oz. sugar into pan, beat whites and shells of 3 eggs, in 2 tablespoonfuls water, add to pan, and stir occasionally till jelly boils. Let it boil well up till it reaches top of pan, draw to one side, and let it stand 10 minutes. Prepare jelly-bag or cheese-cloth by pouring through it 1 quart boiling water, then the jelly. If not clear the first time, pour it back gently into the bag till it runs clear. Pour into small moulds or glasses. After the jelly has been run through the bag, pour in 1½ pints boiling water. Let it run into a jug and stand till cold. It will be a very pleasant drink.

Beef Tea (Slow Method)

Cut 1 pound lean beef (freshly killed meat from top of the round) into thin strips and shred with knife on board. Put in jar with salt and 1 pint cold water, stir well with fork; stand for 2 hours, stirring occasionally to draw out all albumen. Place buttered paper over, to prevent steam condensing and adding to its bulk, and stand in pan of boiling water half-way up jar. Simmer 2½ hours; give final stir when taken out, and strain through coarse strainer, pressing out beef tea with fork.

Jellied Veal

A knuckle of veal   Stalk of celery
½ onion   Salt and pepper
Few slices carrot

Place the veal in boiling water, and simmer until tender, together with the carrot, onion and celery. Remove the veal from the liquid and cool both. When the meat is nearly cold, cut it into tiny cubes, or chop it fine; remove the fat from the broth, reheat the liquid and stir the veal into it, adding salt and pepper, and other seasoning if desired. Pack the hot mixture into a mold, cover with oiled paper, cover and let stand until set. Slice thin and serve cold.

A pioneer woman of Umatilla County, in speaking of those Territorial days remembered them as 'happy days' and days of self-dependence. She recalled there were no bakeries, no laundries and few prepared meats or vegetables. She had little time for club or afternoon parties. *The farm residence of J. J. Adams, Umatilla County, Oregon. Ca 1880.*

Ham and Pork

Boiled Ham

When boiling a ham or a piece of bacon, add a cupful of vinegar and 6 cloves. It will be found to have a most delicious flavour, and especially when cold. Remember also to keep in pot overnight, which also improves flavour. Boil ½ hour to the pound.

Boil charcoal in pot when boiling cabbage, onions, ham and strongly flavoured meat and you will have no smell.

To prepare for serving, dust ham over when lifted from pot with fine bread crumbs, and brown before fire, or strew sugar over the brown. Very good with a mixture of crumbs and sugar.

Curing Hams

To each gallon of water add 1½ pounds of salt, ½ pound of sugar and ⅛ ounce of saltpeter; dissolve saltpeter in a little hot water and mix all together; rub the hams with salt, pack in a well scalded crock, pour on the brine and be sure to weight well and keep all under brine.

Curing Hams

When thoroughly cold after killing, trim them nice and smooth; pack them in salt and let them remain five or six weeks, then dip into boiling brine; rub the flesh side with pulverized black pepper as long as it will stick. Hang in dry place.

To Keep Smoked Hams rub the flesh part with molasses and sprinkle on all the black pepper that will stick. Hang where they will keep dry.

Devilled Ham

Use either the knuckle or any odd bits remaining. Cut off all dark or hard bits and see that at least ¼ of it is fat. Chop very fine, almost to a paste. For a pint of this make dressing of 1 even tablespoonful sugar, 1 even tablespoonful mustard, 1 saltspoonful cayenne pepper, a teacupful good vinegar. Mix sugar, mustard and pepper thoroughly, add vinegar little by little. Stir into chopped ham and pack in small moulds. Pour melted butter over. **Roots of tongue**, same way.

Head Cheese

Use pig's head, ears and tongue. Clean well. Cover with cold salted water and boil until real tender. Strip the meat from the bones. Save part of the tongue to cut up into larger pieces. Chop the rest of the meat extra fine. Season well with salt, pepper, sage, cloves and marjoram. Add one-half cup strong vinegar. Mix all together well. Pack into moulds, alternating the layers with the larger bits of tongue cut into one-inch squares and triangles. Press down and put a wet plate on top and a weight on this. Keep in a cool place. The "cheese" will be ready to use the second day. Turn out of mould and slice. Serve cold with mustard.

Yesler's Cookhouse. Yesler was an early and prominent settler in the Seattle, Washington area and the name will be noticed as one tours the city. *Courtesy of the Seattle Historical Society*

Scrapple

1 hog's head
Salt and pepper
Powdered herbs
Corn-meal
Buckwheat flour

Scrape and clean a hog's head, then split it and take out the eyes and brain. The butcher will do this, if requested. Clean the ears and scrape them well. Put all on to boil in plenty of cold water and simmer gently for four hours, or until the bones will easily slip from the meat. Lift out the meat and bones into a colander, remove the bones and chop the meat fine. Skim off every particle of grease from the water in which the meat was boiled, and return the meat to the boiling stock in the kettle. Season highly with salt and pepper and powdered herbs. Add enough corn-meal and buckwheat flour, in equal quantities, to make a soft mush, stirring constantly for the first fifteen minutes, then lower the heat and cook for one hour. Pour into bread pans, and keep in a cold place until needed.

The scrapple may be served cold or may be cut into slices, dipped in egg and cracker-crumbs and sautéd.

Lamb and Mutton

Mutton Broth

Take a pound of finely chopped lean mutton, including some of the bone, one pint of water and a pinch of salt. Cook for three hours over a slow fire adding water if necessary to make half a pint; then strain through a muslin cloth. When cold, carefully remove the fat adding more salt if necessary. A very nutritious and delicious broth is made from this by adding corn starch or arrowroot, cooking for ten minutes, and then adding three ounces of milk or 1½ ounces of cream to each half pint of broth.

Broth (Sheeps' Head)

One head and trotters thoroughly cleaned and soaked all night in salt and water. Scrape them again next morning, pour a kettleful of boiling water over, and let soak for ½ hour. Put in pot, with 5 or 6 quarts cold water, a teacupful of barley, do. of peas, turnip cut in squares, carrot sliced, leeks or any other vegetables desired. Boil for 3 or 4 hours, season with pepper and salt. Serve broth in tureen, and head and trotters on ashet, garnished with pieces of turnip and carrot. The head may be sprinkled with a few brown bread crumbs and minced parsley, and browned a few minutes in oven. **Forcemeat balls** may be made by mixing the tongue and brains with an equal quantity of fine bread crumbs, pepper and salt, a little minced parsley and 1 egg.

Kidney Pudding

Skin 3 sheep's kidneys, add 1 teaspoon suet, 2 teacups bread crumbs, teaspoon parsley, a very little thyme, and nutmeg, ½ teaspoon sald and ¼ do. pepper. Mix, add 1 beaten egg and 1 teacup milk. Steam in buttered bowl 1 hour. Serve with brown sauce.

Brains on Toast

Soak sheep's or calf's brains in salt water and remove the fibre. Drop into boiling water and simmer 15 minutes. Lift out and remove skin. Chop up and mix with them 2 oz. chopped ham, 2 teaspoonfuls cream, salt, and pepper. Pile up on buttered toast, sprinkle with brown bread crumbs and minced parsley, and serve.

Haggis

Procure the large stomach-bag of a sheep, also one of the smaller bags called "King's Hood", together with the pluck, which is the lights, liver and heart. The bags must be well washed, first in cold water, then plunged in boiling water and scraped. Great care must be taken of the large bag; let it lie and soak in cold water, with a little salt, all night. Wash also the pluck. You will now boil the small bag along with the pluck; in boiling, leave the windpipe attached and let the end of it hang over the edge of the pot, so that impurities may pass freely out. Boil for 1½ hours and take the whole from the pot. When improper. Grate the quarter of the liver (not using the remainder for the haggis) and mince the heart, lights and small bag very small along with ½ pound of beef suet. Mix all this mince with 2 small teacupfuls of oatmeal, previously dried before the fire, black and Jamaica pepper and salt; also add ½ pint of the liquor in which the pluck was boiled, or beef gravy. Stir all together into a consistency. Then take the large bag, which has been thoroughly cleaned, and put the mince into it. Fill it only a little more than half full, in order to leave room for the meal and meat to expand. If crammed too full it will burst in boiling. Sew up the bag with a needle and thread. The haggis is now complete. Put it in a pot with boiling water and prick it occasionally with a large needle, as it swells, to allow the air to escape. If the bag appears thin, tie a cloth outside the skin. There should be a plate beneath it, to prevent it sticking to the bottom of the pot. Boil it for 3 hours. Serve in a napkin on a dish, without garnish or gravy, it being sufficiently rich in itself.

Invalid Jelly

Cut ½ pound each of veal, mutton and the best steak into small pieces and put into a close jar with 2 tablespoonfuls water and pinch of salt. Steam 6 hours. Strain and put into small pots.

Mince Meat (1700's)

To measure, select a medium-sized bowl. Take 5 bowls of apples, 5 bowls of sugar, 2 bowls of raisins, 1 bowl of currants, 1 bowl of mollasses, 1 bowl of vinegar, 1 bowl of butter, 1 bowl of cider and boil until raisins are soft. Then add 3 bowls of meat, 2 tablespoons of cinnamon, 2 tablespoons of cloves, 2 tablespoons nutmeg, 1 tablespoons black pepper, 1 tablespoons salt, and cook until well flavored. Seal in sterilized jars.

In a treeless land, the little Grant girl, mule and sheep escape the hot sun on September 27, 1915. *Courtesy of the Henderson Collection, Washington State University*

Irish Stew

Take 2½ pounds chops from a loin of mutton. Trim off all fat and gristle, cut small, place them in a stewpan with alternate layers of 8 sliced potatoes and of chops and 4 small onions seasoned. Pour 2 breakfastcups water, cover the stewpan closely and let it stew gently until the potatoes are ready to mash and the greater part of the gravy is absorbed. Never lift lid, as that will let out flavour.

Tripe

Lay 1 pound tripe to soak all night in cold water; next day wash it in warm water with a piece of soda in it the size of a pea, but do not let it soak in this, as the soda will harden the tripe. Place the tripe in plenty of cold water, bring to boiling-point; if the water has not a pleasant smell, pour it away, and place the tripe again in cold water, bring again to boiling-point; repeat this until the tripe and water are quite sweet. Then simmer gently for 5 or 6 hours, till the tripe is thoroughly tender. Mix 1 tablespoonful with ½ pint milk, add pepper and a pinch of salt, and ½ pint of the liquor the tripe has been boiled in, bring to boiling point, and boil for 5 minutes.

To Clean Tripe

Wash thoroughly in cold water. Put it in a pot with cold water in which there is a good piece of soda. Let it get hot, but don't allow to boil. Take it out and scrape it white. Let it lie all night in cold water with a little buttermilk in it and next day it will be ready for cooking.

Mincemeat

4 pounds boiled beef, chopped fine
3 pounds beef suet, chopped fine
1½ cups meat stock
Fresh tart apples
6 cups sugar
1 cup molasses
2 quarts apple cider
3 pounds currants
½ pound citron, chopped
1 quart brandy or grape juice
1 teaspoon cinnamon
1 teaspoon allspice
2 teaspoons nutmeg
2 teaspoons cloves
1 teaspoon pepper
1 tablespoon salt
4 pounds raisins, chopped

Chop meat fine. Measure with cup and add 2 times as many cups of chopped apples. Add 5 cups sugar, the molasses, cider, raisins, currants and citron or orange peel and stir well. Add suet, ground as fine as possible, and 1½ cups of meat stock. Heat gradually, stir often and simmer 2 hours. Add spice mixed with remaining 1 cup of sugar and grape juice or brandy. Put into sterilized jars or crocks. Seal or cover with melted paraffin. If brandy is used, add just before sealing. Store mincemeat in a cool place. It improves with age.

Potted Meat

Boil an ox cheek and two calf's feet (fore feet best). Stew slowly until meat comes off bones. Strain and chop meat finely. Season highly with pepper and salt. Mix with the gravy, boil again for ½ hour and then put into moulds. If properly made will keep a week. Or a knuckle of hough (the knee joint) and 3 or 4 pounds of hough. Boil gently, strain, then mince meat finely, season, add mince to gravy, boil 10 minutes and put in moulds.

White Stock

2 pounds chicken or knuckle of veal
1¼ quarts cold water
2 peppercorns
1 clove
½ teaspoon sweet herbs
1 tablespoon, each, of onion and celery
1 teaspoon salt

The liquid in which a fowl or chicken is cooked is also a white stock or chicken broth.

Cracknels

This is what is left from frying out lard. Put them into a pan with a little warm water and some bread crumbs or cold corn bread broken fine. Add pepper and salt. Fry a nice brown and serve hot.

Bone Stock

All kinds of meat, scraps, cooked or uncooked bones (if liver or kidney or rabbit head, soak well in salted water to draw out blood). All kinds of herbs and vegetables, except potatoes (no flour, to keep stock clear). Bring 1 quart cold water to 1 pound of bones, salt and pepper quickly to a boil with lid off. Skim thoroughly and simmer very slowly all day and even all night. Strain.

To Clarify Dripping

Put dripping from the roast (either mutton or beef) in pan with a little water to cover the bottom of pan. Let dripping thoroughly dissolve. Pour into basin and stand all night. In the morning it will be caked. Lift out cake of dripping, and melt it in pan. Pour into jars. Twist paper round, and set away. Keeps splendidly.

To Clarify Suet

Place in large stewpan minced suet, skin and fat of all kinds, with 1 pint water. Stir constantly and when froth rises skim. It is ready when water is evaporated and fat is quite brown. Strain, when it is ready for use.

Fish

Fish Balls (Norwegian)

Using ½ pound Haddock, scrape from the bone and pound in mortar till fine. Boil the bones and keep extract; season with pepper and salt, and grated nutmeg; add a small piece of butter about the size of a walnut. Boil ½ teacupful of cream and let it cool, then pour it among fish and flavouring. Make into balls and cook in extract or boiling fat. Serve with white sauce coloured pink.

Trout

Large trout are good for grilling, which can be done in several ways. The fish can be cleaned, wiped, rubbed over with oiled butter and placed on a gridiron over a very clear fire, being turned several times in the process of cooking.

Curried Fish

Fry 2 pound Cod, or other fish in 2 oz. butter, remove it, then fry 1 onion brown, add ½ tablespoon curry powder and fry slightly; then add 1 tablespoonful cocoanut, ½ pint stock, a dust of sugar and salt and boil 15 minutes; divide the fish into large flakes, add to curry, and boil 15 minutes, then add lemon juice.

To Kipper Salmon

Lay the fish on a board and cover with ¼ pound best brown sugar, 1 pound salt, 2 oz. powdered saltpetre, ¼ pound black pepper, and a little allspice. Lay aside for 3 days. Dry in the sun, and it is ready for use.

Baked Lake Trout

Clean fish, rub inside and out, with vinegar. Make dressing same as for turkey, stuff the fish and tie with cord, sprinkle with flour and place bits of butter over it. Bake one hour. For the sauce as follows: Stir till smooth and thick 1 pint sweet milk, 2 tablespoons flour. When cold add cup of sweet cream. Pepper and salt to taste.

Trout

Small-sized trout are best fried. Clean them and wipe them dry with a cloth—a soft cloth and a gentle hand are necessary. Then dredge them lightly with flour, or roll in fine oatmeal. Melt enough dripping in your frying pan to just cover the fish; when it is still and smoking, put in the fish one at a time, with a few seconds between each, so as to keep up the heat of the friture. Fry a golden-brown, take up, sprinkle with salt, drain on thickly folded kitchen paper in front of the fire and serve—a good appetite is the only sauce needed.

Whiting (Fried)

Skin the whitings; remove the gills and eyes; dry them thoroughly and draw the tails through the eyes. Roll in flour and brush over with egg. Put into a basket, with enough smoking fat to cover. Fry gently 5 minutes, a nice brown. Drain on soft paper. Dish in a ring and garnish with parsley, fried; serve with sauce.

The coming of the Northern Pacific Railroad was celebrated with a salmon barbecue which was held at the site of the present University of Washington Campus, September 16, 1883. *Courtesy of the Seattle Historical Society*

The bleakness of prairie homestead life is revealed in this 1912 picture of the J. S. Hedrick Ranch. *Courtesy of Washington State University Library, Henderson Collection*

On the Fred Renz place in June of 1911, the photographer has focused his camera on the entire family and farm creatures. No doubt grain was scattered to keep the chickens and cow from moving about. This picture and the others of the series were made on glass negatives.

Game/Fowl

Roast Game

Truss, dust with flour and put inside a piece of butter rolled in pepper and salt. Place on a rack in a tin with some butter and baste well with the butter every 7 to 10 minutes all the time the bird is cooking; about ½ hour for a partridge. For woodcock or snipe 15 or 20 minutes is long enough.

When cooked have ready a piece of toast buttered on one side. Lift the bird from the tin. Pour the fat away, but keep back the sediment in the tin and put it on the hot toast to flavour it. Place the bird on the toast and it is ready to serve with chipped potatoes and brown bread crumbs, handed separately.

Roasted Wild Duck

Clean a wild duck for roasting. Paraffin added to the scalding water aids greatly in this task. Truss and soak in cold water one hour. This draws out the blood and whitens the meat. Drain and wipe dry then sprinkle generously, inside and out, with salt and pepper. In the meantime cook 1 cupful of wild rice in salted boiling water until tender. Drain, rinse, and drain again. Melt 4 tablespoonfuls of butter or ham fryings in a skillet, add 1 small onion cut fine and the giblets which have been cooked tender. Mix and cook slowly for a few minutes, then add the rice. Season to taste with salt and pepper and stuff the duck. Place the fowl in a roaster and strip with bacon or salt pork. Place in a hot oven of 450 degrees and bake until it begins to brown, then reduce the heat and allow 20 to 30 minutes per pound. The time depends upon the age of the duck. Baste the fowl occasionally with hot water or the juice that forms in the bottom of the pan and do not allow the pan to become dry. Do not overcook wild duck for this tends to dry it out.

Roast Duck and Goose (Domestic or Wild Ducks or Goose)

Singe the ducks and remove the pin feathers, wash and scrub in hot water (if a goose use hot soap suds) then draw (that is the intestines removed and tendons pulled out). Wash in cold water by holding under the faucet, wipe dry and truss. Place the ducks in the baking pan, preferably one with a rack in the bottom, and cover the breast with very thin slices of bacon or salt pork. Bake in a very hot oven fifteen minutes to every pound if wild ducks and little more than twice the time if domestic. Add half a cup of boiling water for each duck and baste every ten minutes. Serve onions and brussel sprouts or browned sweet potatoes, apple and celery salad or lettuce and orange salad.

Roast Goose

Prepare same as for duck and rub the inside with salt and an onion cut in halves. Fill with prune stuffing and steam for two hours and bake one hour, basting every ten minutes.

Roast Goose

Prepare 1 medium-sized goose, stuff the body of the bird well with sage and onion stuffing, then tie the ends of the legs together. Cover with fat and roast slowly, allowing 12 minutes to each pound. If not browning sufficiently well, dredge over with flour in the last ½ hour. When done, pour the fat from the tin, add to what is left 1 tablespoonful flour, ½ pint good stock made from the giblets, salt and pepper. Boil up, pour a little round the goose and serve the remainder in a tureen. Serve with apple sauce.

Pigeon Pie

If to be eaten hot, have nice flaky crust. If intended cold, short crust, preferably, and should be equally rich or nearly so. Butter dish and lay crust round sides and round edges. At bottom of dish place a fine beef-steak, seasoned with pepper and salt, then the birds rubbed with pepper and salt inside and out and a piece of butter in each. Some add the liver chopped up, with parsley. Observe to lay the breasts downwards to keep them juicy. A bit of ham is sometimes laid on each pigeon and a hard-boiled egg between every two, but neither of these is necessary. Put ½ pint gravy and have ready a little more to pour in boiling hot at top when cooked. Season the gizzards and, if you cut them off, two joints of the pinions and lay in middle of dish. Lay on top crust and make hole in centre, wherein may be stuck some of the feet, nicely cleaned. Brush over with beaten yolk of egg and back 1½ hours if not very large.

Hasenpfeffer

After the rabbit has been in salt water for several hours, rinse with clear water. Boil until tender in water containing an onion in which are stuck about a dozen cloves. When tender take from liquor, roll in flour and fry brown in skillet, using equal quantities of butter and lard; just before removing from skillet, sprinkle over a little cinnamon and about 1 tablespoonful of vinegar (more or less to suit taste); cook closely; let smother for a few minutes; remove rabbit; put flour in skillet and brown in remaining grease; add liquor in which the rabbit was cooked to make a nice gravy; pour over rabbit.

Rabbit Stew

Cut up the rabbit, cover with cold water and put over the fire; add a teaspoonful of salt and boil until tender. Have ready hot biscuits broken open and laid on a platter and on each place a piece of the rabbit. Thicken the gravy with 2 tablespoonfuls of flour wet smoothly in a little milk; let it boil a minute, then add a cup of milk or cream and stir well. Pour this over the rabbit and biscuit and serve at once.

A frontiersman stressed, in providing food for the larder, that 'each male person should have at least one rifle gun and a shot gun is also very useful for wild fowl and small game, of which there is an abundance—hare, rabbit, grouse, sage hen, pheasant and quail.' The larger game consisted of elk, deer, antelope, mountain sheep and bear. *Courtesy of the Seattle Historical Society*

Game/Venison

To Roast Venison

It is such a dry meat, venison requires great care in cooking and longer time than mutton. Baste a 4 pound venison first with ½ pint milk or cream and when this is absorbed add 3 oz. drippings and baste very often. When cooked, lift the venison to a hot dish, pour away the fat, leaving the sediment in the pan. Add to this 1 gill stock, pepper and salt and one teaspoonful red-currant jelly. Stir all till boiling and strain over venison. Serve very hot with red-currant jelly. Venison is very tasty browned and roasted in pan over fire—just cooked slowly with a little water—no basting needed.

Venison Sauerbraten

Mix 2 cups vinegar, 2 cups water, 2 onions, sliced, 2 Tablespoons salt, 2 Tablespoons sugar, 1 lemon sliced, 10 cloves, 4 bay leaves, 6 whole peppers, or pepper to taste, and pour over 4 pound roast, rump or sirloin tip, place in a cool place. Turn every once in a while and leave for 24 to 36 hours. Cover meat. After soaking for the above time, take out roast and flour it well. Brown in heavy kettle, add 1 cup marinade and put on lid. Cook at moderate heat. When roast is done remove and thicken gravy and serve. More marinade may be used in the gravy or if you don't want too spicy a taste, use water.

Venison Steak

Cut steak thin and pound flour into steak—all the meat will retain. Have a heavy skillet hot with enough shortening to keep meat from burning. Brown well and quickly—do not overcook. As the meat cooks, the juices will ooze through the flour coating, sprinkle these places generously with more flour so no juice escapes. When meat is brown on both sides, pour over a cup of cream. The flour will thicken the gravy which should be thin. Serve at once with hot biscuits or, better still, hot cakes.

Game is garnished with barbarries, red-currant jelly, or rowan jelly.

Henry Reimann bagged 28 rabbits on January 15, 1911. "A three-hour hunt by moonlight." *Courtesy Henderson Collection, Washington State University Library*

A successful hunter in the Yakima area of Washington State poses with deer and dog on November 12, 1893. *Courtesy of the Seattle Historical Society*

Soups

Bone Soup

Bones cooked or uncooked, but it is better not to mix raw and cooked bones. Break them and put in sauce pan with 1½ pints cold water to every 1 pound of bone. Boil 4 hours at least. Strain. Then put in carrot, turnip and onions, cut small; parsley, herbs, and ¼ pound rice, pepper, salt. Boil another hour.

Hough or Shin Soup

Take marrow from bone of 2 pound Hough (shin of beef), and place in pot with 4 pints water. When hot, put in meat cut small, and simmer 5 min., stirring occasionally. Add water and onions cut small, salt and pepper, and boil 3 hours. (This same recipe without the onions and a knap-bone added makes a good potted meat.)

Leek Soup

Melt 2 oz. dripping in pan. Stir 1 pound potatoes, thinly sliced, 4 good-sized Leeks, cut in slices of 2 inches thick, and 1 stick of white part of celery cut into dice, in this with a wooden spoon for 5 minutes, but do not brown. Sprinkle over vegetables ½ teaspoonful pepper and teaspoonful salt. Add 2 pints stock or water. Simmer gently 1½ hours. Cut small dice of toast, put into tureen, and pour soup over.

Lentil Soup

Soak ½ pint lentils (Egyptian) the previous night. Boil them, and a good-sized onion, in sufficient water to cover them, till tender, and pass through sieve. Thicken 1 pint milk or stock with the flour, and add to the lentils with salt, pepper, ½ teaspoon of curry powder and a lump of sugar, and bring all to the boil and serve hot.

Lentil, Pea, Barley and Rice Soup

In 4 quarts stock or water, add 1 teacup each of lentils, split peas, barley and rice, 1 oz. of dripping, a carrot and turnip, grated and 1 Spanish onion, minced finely. Boil 3 hours.

Lentil and Rice Soup (Very Nourishing)

Soak ¾ teacup of lentils 24 hours, after washing them well. Boil lentils, in 2 quarts water, add 2 onions, chopped fine, 1 carrot grated, 2 tablespoonfulls minced parsley, and ½ teacup rice, and boil all 1½ hours. Add salt and pepper. A little mutton boiled in it, or Lemco added, is an improvement.

Mulligatawny

Cut one onion in rings and 1 oz. ham into small dice. Make the 1 oz. butter hot in the pan the soup is to be made in. Fry the onion and ham, and when brown add 1 turnip, small piece carrot, 1 small apple, ½ teaspoonful curry paste, 1 teaspoonful curry powder, and 1 quart stock. Let all simmer 1 hour, then strain through a hair sieve. Mix a tablespoonful flour with cold water, stir into the soup, and keep stirring till it boils.

Ox-Tail Soup

Cut an ox tail in pieces. Slice 3 onions, and cut 1 carrot, and 1 turnip, into dice. Put 2 oz. dripping in frying-pan, and stir in 2 oz. flour as dripping melts. Then put in vegetables and stir for 5 minutes. Add meat, and fry for 10 minutes, stirring occasionally. Turn all into pot with 3 quarts water and simmer 3 hours, skimming well. About an hour before serving put in shreds of tops of stalk of celery, a little thyme (either dried or fresh), pepper and salt. May be strained and thickened with 1 tablespoonful flour. Serve small pieces of tail in the soup, and, if liked, add a little Yorkshire relish at the last.

Poultry Soup

Skin and entirely clean out the insides of three fat fowls; let them be well washed in warm water; put them into a pan for an hour, covered with strong veal broth, and add a good-sized bunch of parsley. Take the crumbs of two French rolls and soak them in the liquor; cut the meat off, take away the skin, and pound the flesh in a mortar, adding the soaked crumbs and the yolks of 4 hard-boiled eggs; force this through a coarse sieve, and put it into a quart of cream that has been previously boiled; rewarm for table. The proportions are for a dozen people.

Thickening for Soup

1 oz. arrowroot. Add sufficient liquid to make a consistency of batter, and quite smooth. Pour into the boiling soup. Stir quickly, and simmer 10 minutes. 1 oz. arrowroot to 1 quart soup.

Croutons for Soup

Cut some bread ¼ inch thick; stamp out in rounds. Put ¼ pound butter into a pan, and melt; pour off the top into a frying-pan, and make it a light brown. Throw in the bread, and fry a golden colour. Drain on soft paper, and serve.

John Wagness with gun and ducks. *Courtesy of the Seattle Historical Society*

MISCELLANEOUS RECEIPTS

Flavouring Spices

Dry 1 oz. each of bay leaves, marjoram, sweet basil, thyme, ground cloves, white pepper, ground mace and nutmeg carefully in the sun, pull off stalks. Rub through hair sieve and bottle for use. Excellent for forcemeats, stews, soups, etc.

Horse Radish Sauce

To one cup grated horse radish add the following dressing—two-thirds of vinegar, one-fourth cup of sugar, one level teaspoon salt, one teaspoon olive oil. Warm this mixture but do not allow it to get hot. Pour over the grated root, mix well and cool.

French Mustard

Put on plate 1 oz. best powdered mustard, 1 saltspoon salt, a few leaves tarragon, and 1 clove of garlic minced fine. Pour it on by degrees sufficient vinegar to dilute to proper consistency, about ½ gill. Mix with wooden spoon, and don't use it in less than 24 hours.

Nasturtium Seeds (Substitute for capers.)

Gather seeds before too old, put in salt and water 24 hours, then rub dry and put in bottle. Boil ½ pint vinegar and 1 teaspoonful peppercorns and strain it. When cold put in bottles with nasturtiums, adding more as they are ready; afterwards seal bottles. Will keep a year.

Whether using log, planed lumber or sod, building a home was a requisite in complying with the Homestead Act. There were seldom any frills and many of the homes were unpainted. This picture was taken of the Ridgeway place near Quincy, Washington and the scene is typical of the more arid lands of the West. *Courtesy of the Henderson Collection, Washington State Library*

Breads and Cereals

The pleasant nature of this early trade card does not reflect the struggle of farming in a raw, new land. The squirrels took crops. Hand flails or horses and oxen were used to thresh their grain. It took two months or more to harvest grain crops. *Courtesy of the Seattle Historical Society*

To Bake Breads

A moderate, uniform heat is very necessary in baking bread. If the heat is too great a hard crust is quickly formed before the bread has expanded sufficiently and it will be heavy. If the bare hand and arm can be held in the oven not longer than enough to count twenty moderately, it is hot enough. Or, it may be tested by placing a small quantity of flour in the center of the oven on an old piece of crockery; if it browns in one minute the heat is right.

To tell when the bread is done break the loaves apart and press gently with the finger; if elastic, it is done, but if clammy, it needs to be returned to the oven. Or the loaves may be tested with a broom splint. If nothing adheres when it is withdrawn the bread is done.

Beer Yeast

For 1 gallon of yeast, take 12 medium-size potatoes, pare and boil them until done. With the water off these, scald 3 heaping tablespoonfuls of flour, 3 tablespoons of sugar, and 3 scant tablespoonfuls of salt. Mix the potatoes, mashed, with this, then fill gallon with cold water. When cold enough, add 1 cake of magic yeast. Let stand in cool place. Take 1 pint of mixture for 1 loaf of bread.

Hop Yeast

On one morning boil two ounces of the best hops in four quarts of water half an hour; strain it, and let the liquor cool to the consistency of new milk; then put it in an earthen bowl and add half a cupful of salt and half a cupful of brown sugar; beat up one quart of flour with some of the liquor; then mix all well together; and let it stand till the third day after; then add six medium-sized potatoes boiled and mashed through a colander; let it stand a day, then strain and bottle and it is fit for use.

It must be stirred frequently while it is making and kept near a fire. One advantage of this yeast is its spontaneous fermentation, requiring the help of no old yeast; if care be taken to let it ferment well in the bowl, it may immediately be corked tightly. Keep it in a cool place. Before using it shake the bottle up well. It will keep in a cool place two months, and is best the latter part of the time.

Hop Yeast

Take 1 quart of hops, boiled and strained, 1 cup of sugar, ½ cup of salt, ½ cup of lard, 2 large tablespoonfuls of ginger, 4 potatoes boiled and mashed and enough yeast to raise it. Let stand over night, then mix enough flour and corn meal to make crumbly.

Potato Yeast

Boil enough potatoes to make one pint when mashed very fine. Save potato water and add enough more water to make 3 pints, then add 1 tablespoonful salt and ½ cup sugar and 1 cake compressed yeast, put in the potatoes and stir well, cover and let rise over night. In the morning save 1 pint for next baking or make fresh each time, as desired; mix stiffer with flour than with other yeast.

Potato Yeast

Boil and mash three potatoes. Add ¼ cup of sugar and ½ cup of flour and ½ tablespoonful of salt; stir well together. Pour over this mixture ½ pint of boiling water and stir it; then add ½ pint of cold water and stir that; then ½ cup of yeast and keep it in a warm place. When it is risen well and rounds up to the top of the dish stir it down. Do so several times during the day. Then it may be strained and put into a jar or jug, and kept in a cool place. The bread made with this may be made with milk.

Baking Powder

Four ounces tartaric acid, 5 ounces bulk soda, 1 pint flour; sift all together four times.

Salt Rising Bread

Scald one cup of milk and allow it to cool until it is luke-warm; then add 1 tablespoonful sugar, 2 tablespoons white corn-meal and salt. If lard is used add 1 tablespoonful. Place in a fruit can or a heavy crock or pitcher and surround by water as hot as you can stand your hand in. This temperature can be secured by mixing equal parts of boiling water and cold water. Allow the mixture to stand for six or seven hours, or until it shows signs of fermentation. When it is fermented enough the gas can be heard as it escapes. This leaven contains enough liquid for one loaf. If more loaves are needed, add 1 cup water, 1 teaspoon salt, 1 teaspoon sugar and 1 tablespoon of lard for each additional loaf to be made. Beat thoroughly and put the sponge again at the temperature of about 120 degrees. When it is very light, add more flour gradually until the dough is so stiff that it can be kneaded without sticking to the hands. Knead ten or fifteen minutes; put into pans and let it rise until two and one-half its bulk and bake. This bread is not as light as bread raised with yeast.

Those who crossed the plains with the intention of farming a homestead were advised to take along a few plow moulds 'as it is difficult getting such articles—plows costing from twenty-five to forty dollars each' according to wagonmaster General Joel Palmer who led 3,000 emigrants across the country in 1845. *Courtesy of the Seattle Historical Society*

Cutting oats on the Engbretsen farm near Norman, Washington in 1907. This farm implement is called a mowing machine, and has long since been replaced with more sophisticated equipment. Not visible is the long sickle or bar with moving 'teeth' which extends to the left just above ground level and mows the crop as the machine is pulled forward. *Courtesy of the Seattle Historical Society*

Baking Powder

A scant pint of flour, ½ pound of soda and a pound of best cream of tartar. Sift together eight times through a flour sieve. Fill tin boxes and cover tightly.

Baking Powder

Six ounces cream of tartar, 2⅔ ounce bicarbonate of soda, 4½ ounces of flour. It is claimed this is the recipe from which is made one of the most popular brands of baking powder on the market.

Baking-Powder

Take equal weights of rice flour, bicarbonate of soda and powdered tartaric acid; mix thoroughly, pass through a sieve, and keep in tins for use. For pastry, use 1 teaspoonful to 1 pound flour; for cakes, 2 teaspoonfuls to 1 pound flour.

Beaten Bisquits

Take one quart of flour, one cooking spoon lard, salt to taste and mix as for a pie crust. Put it through a meat grinder several times, then beat it till it blisters. Bake slowly.

Self-Raising Flour

Put half-a-stone of flour into a basin; mix with the flour 1½ oz. bicarbonate of soda, and exactly the same weight of cream of tartar. Add also 3 teaspoonfulls of fine salt and 1 tablespoon fine sugar. Mix and pass through wire sieve, or very carefully with the hand. Will keep good in a covered crock for weeks. In winter when the buttermilk is not so acid, 2 oz. cream of tartar will be required for 1½ oz. of soda. For 4 teacupfuls of this prepared flour, add 1 breakfastcup of buttermilk; a dessert-spoon of butter rubbed into the flour is a great improvement.

Dried Yeast and Yeast Cakes

To make dried yeast and yeast cakes make a pan of yeast, the same as homemade yeast. Mix in with it cornmeal that has been sifted and dried, kneading it well until it is thick enough to roll out, and to cut into cakes or crumble up. Spread out and dry thoroughly in the shade; keep in a dry place.

Corn Bread

Mix 1 cupful yellow Indian meal, ½ do. flour, 2 heaped teaspoonfuls baking-powder, ½ do. salt and 1 do. sugar. Rub in 1 level tablespoonful of butter; add the beaten yolks of 2 eggs, 1¼ cupfuls milk; beat in the beaten whites of the eggs, and bake in a hot oven about ½ hour.

Corn Pone

Two eggs, ½ cup of shortening, 1¼ cups of sugar, 1 cup of corn meal, 2 teaspoonfuls baking powder and milk to make light cake batter. Bake in slow oven.

Gingerbread

Mix 1 pound flour, 4 oz. butter, 4 oz. peel and currants, 3 oz. ground sugar, ½ oz. spice, 2 eggs, ½ pound treacle, and moisten with buttermilk. Bake in moderate oven for nearly 1 hour.

Soft Ginger Bread

Combine the following ingredients. ½ cup of sugar, ½ cup of butter, 1 tablespoon ginger, 2 well beaten eggs, 3 cups flour, 1 cup molasses, 1 cup boiling water, 2 teaspoons cinnamon, 3 teaspoons soda. Raisins may also be added.

Indian Fried Bread or Sheepherders Dough Gods

This bread is usually made in the top of a sack full of flour. Scoop out a hole and put in about 2 teaspoons sugar and ⅔ cup of milk or water. Stir around with the fingers and knead just until it holds together. Pinch off a small amount to make a patted three-inch circle. Fry in a skillet in hot oil about 1 inch deep. Serve hot with Huckleberry Jam.

Spoon Bread

¼ cup of fat and cracklings from pork, beef, or chicken fat
3 cups boiling water
½ teaspoon salt
1 cup corn-meal
2 eggs

Add fat and cracklings to the water, and when boiling sprinkle in the salt and corn-meal, stirring constantly. Cook in a double boiler one hour, cool, and add the well-beaten eggs. Turn into a greased baking-dish and bake in a moderate oven (350 degrees F.) three-fourths of an hour.

Squaw Bread

1 pint sour milk
1 tablespoon lard
¼ teaspoon soda
3 heaping teaspoons baking powder
½ teaspoon salt
Flour enough to make a dough easily handled

Knead smooth, roll to ½ inch thickness. Divide in portions equal to a medium size biscuit. Cut 3 or 4 slits in each and cook in deep fat as for doughnuts. This should make a piece about the size of a saucer.

Courtesy of the Seattle Historical Society

Apple Pancakes

Any ordinary pancake batter will do for this dish. Make your pancakes very thin in small frying-pan. As you fry, place them on one another, and cover to keep hot. Have ready, previously made, about a breakfast-cupful of apple pulp, made with well-flavoured apples and sugar. No spice or water required in making the pulp; merely pare, quarter and core your apples. Put them into a small saucepan over a gentle heat until soft; then with a silver fork heat into a pulp. Now take a pancake. Put a spoonful of pulp in the centre; fold over to make a square. The pulp cannot fall out if folded properly. When all are ready, lay them on a dish, cover over, and put in the oven till quite hot. When ready to serve, sprinkle over with castor sugar and a little powdered cinnamon. Serve quickly.

Noodles

Beat one egg, add to it enough flour as needed to roll out thin. Cut into very fine strips and boil in soup. Noodles made by above directions boiled in milk, make a very palatable dish, especially for a delicate appetite.

Hush Puppies

1 cup cornmeal
½ cup flour (all-purpose)
1½ teaspoon baking powder
½ teaspoon salt
1 egg
1 cup milk
1 finely crushed garlic

Sift meal, flour, baking powder, salt and add garlic. Beat egg, add egg and milk to meal mixture and stir until well mixed. Let stand for 5 minutes, add more milk if needed. (Mixture should be thin enough to drop from spoon.) Drop by small spoonfuls in hot fat. Fry until golden brown. Serves four.

Barley Water

Pour 1 pint boiling water over 2 oz. barley, 1 oz. sugar, rind and juice of 1 lemon. Set in same manner as apple water.

Noodles

Mix 1 egg, pinch of salt, with flour as stiff as can be rolled and roll thin. Let stand two hours. Roll up and cut in threads. Boil 20 minutes. Drain and pour browned butter over them and serve.

Men in the field with two grain binders. After the grain was bound into bundles it was gathered into 'shocks' by hand, then loaded on wagons and hauled to a threshing machine which separated the straw from the grain. *Courtesy of the Seattle Historical Society*

Gonoquis

Gonquis are the dainty French version of what they call "dumplings" in England. To make them, bring to a boil one cupful of milk, add six tablespoonfuls of flour smoothed in a very little cold milk, and stir all until the mixture is so thick that it can be formed into balls. Take the pan off the fire and keep beating constantly while adding the yolks of two eggs, one after the other. Beat the first egg yolk in well before adding the second so that the paste is not thinned at all. Then add one-quarter pound of grated cheese, half a teaspoonful of salt and one-eighth teaspoonful of pepper. Have ready a pan of boiling salted water such as would be used for poaching eggs. Take up the paste in wee lumps between two teaspoons and drop them into the boiling water. When they rise to the top they are done. Take them up with a skimmer, draining them very well, and lay them in a large flat dish. Pour over them enough well seasoned medium thick white sauce to coat them well—about one cupful. Sprinkle the surface with grated cheese and brown in a hot oven or under a broiler flame. If wished, the cheese may be omitted when making the paste and the gonoquis served quite plain with tomato sauce or a good brown gravy. For visitors, use a little sugar instead of any other flavoring and pour hot sirup around them in the dish. They make a fascinating pudding.

Bran Tea or Soup

Wash 4 handfuls bran and boil in 2 quarts water 1½ hours slowly. Strain and put liquid in clean pan with 3 good-sized tomatoes cut up. Boil together for ½ hour and strain again. Take a teacupful as a restorative in the forenoon.

Cooked Grain

To cook grain without stirring, put the rice or other grain in tin canister (preferable to earthenware, because tin is a good conductor of heat) with a tight-fitting lid. Set in saucepan with boiling water ¾ up tin. Cover, and keep water boiling fast till grain is cooked. If no canister is handy, a mould or cake-tin will do, covered with plate or greased paper twisted tightly round. Room must be left for grain to swell, and a little butter will hasten the cooking.

Gruel

Put 1 tablespoonful oatmeal in basin and pour ½ pint cold water over. Let it soak 20 or 30 minutes. Then with a spoon press all the flour from the oatmeal, and pour into the pan, leaving meal as dry as possible. Keep stirring till it boils. Boil very slowly, with a pinch of salt, for 15 or 20 minutes. You may use milk instead of water to cook it, or half milk and water. If butter is allowed, you may put it in basin before you pour gruel in; or if you want sweet gruel, put sugar in before pouring gruel in.

Water gruel or weak tea assists perspiration; milk and coffee retard it.

Hominy Porridge

Soak ½ pound hominy all night in 1 pint cold water, then cook for 1½ hours in a double pan with the water it was soaked in, also 1 pint milk. Just before serving stir in 1 oz. butter. Serve with golden syrup.

Porridge

Soak 4 oz. oatmeal overnight in ½ pint water, then cook in a double pan for about 1½ hours in the morning with ½ pint milk. A small piece of butter may be mixed in before serving.

Spoon Bread

1 cup cornmeal	2 tablespoons melted butter
2 tablespoons all-purpose flour	2 eggs
1 teaspoon salt	2 teaspoons baking powder
2½ cup milk	

Combine cornmeal, flour and salt in a large bowl. Scald milk; stir slowly into cornmeal mixture. Beat well to prevent lumping. Add butter and eggs; beat until smooth. Sprinkle baking powder over surface; beat in quickly. Pour into greased 1½ quart casserole. Bake in 350 degrees F. oven 30 to 35 minutes. Serve at once. Number of servings—6.

The entire family joins the grain harvesters late in the September afternoon of 1911. The horse drawn combine is operating on the Overbay place. *Courtesy of Washington State University, Henderson Collection*

BEVERAGES

Coffee

One cup of medium ground coffee, one egg, one cup cold water, put in coffee pot and shake well. Put all on stove and let come to a boil. Add two quarts of boiling water, and boil from three to five minutes.

Elder-Flower Water

When elders are in flower, gather them on a dry day—full but fresh blossoms. Put flowers in preserving-pan with sufficient water to cover them, and boil ½ hour. Strain, and stand till cold. Put in pan with ½ pound sugar to each pint of the flavoured water. Boil 10 minutes, skimming well all the time. Bottle when cold, corking bottles tight and sealing down. For the ordinary shape of rice, etc., use a breakfast-cupful, and make as usual, but using less sugar.

Kentucky Egg Nog

Stir ⅔ of a cup of sugar into 6 eggs that have been beaten until light. When dissolved add 12 tablespoonfuls of best whiskey. The whiskey is intended to cook the egg and the quantity used depends upon its strength. Mix a pint of rich cream with the other ingredients. This makes 6 glasses of egg nog. Grate a little nutmeg over the top of each glass when filled.

Farmer's Soda

Strain the juice of a lemon and put into a medium sized tumbler; after adding a tablespoonful of powdered sugar, fill the tumbler ⅔ full of cold water; stir until the sugar is dissolved, then add a teaspoonful of soda, stir and drink while effervescing.

Unfermented Grape Wine

Pick only the perfectly sound berries from the stems of a twenty pound basket of ordinary blue grapes. Crush with potato masher and put them over a brisk fire in a granite or bright tin preserving pan (not an old tin or iron pot) with a cupful or two of water to prevent burning, and scald until the skins and pulp separate. Then pour into a flannel bag wrung out of hot water and let drip. When it has stopped running, empty the pulp into another basin, mix it thoroughly with a quart or so of boiling water, and let drip again. Do not squeeze the bag, it only makes the grape juice muddy and stains your hands. Wash your kettle, put your juice on with two to four pounds of white sugar, (some people like it sweeter than others), bring it rapidly to just a scalding heat, skim it thoroughly, bottle and seal at once with wax. The bottles should be heated in a kettle of hot water.

Oatmeal Drink

When placed by the side of any alcoholic drink it shows itself infinitely superior, and much cheaper. Take of fine oatmeal ¼ pound, coarse sugar ¼ pound; ground ginger ½ oz.; essence of lemon 30 drops; boiling water 1 gallon. Pour the boiling water over the other ingredients, stirring well all the time, then boil the whole for about 3 minutes. A thicker and more nourishing drink can be made by adding ½ or ¾ pound of oatmeal to the gallon of water.

Miss Annie Larson of Salmon Bay, Washington pours coffee in this charming camera study made in the early 1900s. *Courtesy of the Seattle Historical Society*

Peppermint Cordial

Simmer 1 pound loaf sugar and 1 pint boiling water 10 minutes, then stir in 1 tablespoonful honey. When nearly cold, add 30 drops of the essence of peppermint. Bottle for use. 4 tablespoonfuls to a tumbler of hot or cold water makes a delicious drink. Essence of ginger can be used in the same way.

Cottage Beer

Put a peck of good wheat bran and 3 handfuls of hops into 10 gallons of water and boil together until the bran and hops sink to the bottom. Then strain it through a thin cloth into a cooler and add 2 quarts of molasses when it is about lukewarm. As soon as the molasses is dissolved, pour the mixture into a ten-gallon cask and add 2 tablespoonfuls of yeast. When fermentation is over with, cork up the cask and it will be ready for use in four or five days.

Ginger Beer

Add 6 ounces of bruised ginger to 3 quarts of water and boil for 30 minutes; add 5 pounds of loaf sugar, ¼ pound of honey, a gill of lemon juice and 17 quarts more of water; strain through a cloth and when it is cold, add 2 drachms of essence of lemon and the whole of an egg. Bottle after standing for 3 or 4 days.

Hop Beer

Take five quarts of water, six ounces of hops and boil the mixture three hours. Strain the liquor and to it add five quarts of water and four ounces of bruised ginger roots. Boil again twenty minutes, strain and add four pounds of sugar. When lukewarm, a pint of yeast is put in. Let the beer ferment for 24 hours and bottle.

Spruce Beer

For each gallon of water add an ounce of hops and a spoonful of ginger well boiled and strained. Add a pint of molasses or a pound of brown sugar and half an ounce of essence of spruce. When cool add a teacupful of yeast, put into a clean, tight cask, ferment for a day or two and bottle. Sprigs of spruce fir can be boiled in place of the essence.

Camomile Tea

1 tablespoonful of the dried flowers to a cup boiling water. Pour water over. Cover and steep by side of fire 10 minutes or so. Good for sleeplessness.

Linseed Tea

Put into a saucepan 1 tablespoonful of whole linseed, pour on it 2 breakfastcupfuls of water, and boil from 25 to 35 minutes. Strain it and sweeten with honey or sugar, and add the juice of a lemon.

Blackberry Wine

First measure the berries and bruise them; add 1 quart of boiling water to each gallon; let the mixture stand 24 hours stirring occasionally; then strain off the liquor and put into a cask; to every gallon add 2 pound of sugar; cork tight and let stand till the next October, when it will be ready for use. It may be bottled if desired.

This old trade card provides an insight beyond the samples of tinware, a necessity carried along with families coming West over the old pioneer trails. *Courtesy of the Seattle Historical Society*

Planting grain in the early 1900s required many men and teams of horses. The extra men needed during planting and harvesting were fed in a mess tent by girls or women hired to prepare meals for the crew. The picture was taken in April of 1916.
Courtesy of the Henderson Collection, Washington State University Library

Elderberry Wine

Pick the elderberries when dead ripe and extract 5 quarts juice with a fruit press. Into the keg put the above amount of juice dissolved in water, and 15 pounds sugar. Be sure the sugar is thoroughly dissolved before putting it into the keg. Fill the remaining space with water. Rack off in February and wash keg in which you can replace the clear wine or it can be bottled. This makes a heavy sweet wine on the order of port. To make it more tart and without so much body use four quarts of juice and fourteen pounds of sugar. The first wine is dark colored while the latter is lighter in color. To make the wine from the elderberry blossoms pick when dead ripe and falling from the bush; pick from the stems and to one quart of blossoms add the juice of two lemons, four pounds of sugar and pour over all one gallon of boiling water.

Let cool and when lukewarm add one half yeast cake to five gallons of wine and let ferment three days. Put into a keg, leave hung out, and let ferment for a month or six weeks. When through with fermentation it can be racked off and bottled.

Elder Blossom Wine

Add 1 gallon of boiling water to 1 quart of elder blossoms and let stand 1 hour; then strain and add 3 pounds of sugar; boil a little and skim. Let stand until lukewarm; then add 1 lemon, sliced fine, and 1 tablespoonful good yeast. Let stand 24 hours. Then strain and put into bottles or jugs, filling full until all impurities are worked out. Be sure to fill up jugs as fast as it works out, and the wine will be a beautiful amber color. In making this wine, great care should be taken to keep all stems out, as they make the wine taste rank and give it a dark color.

Honey Wine

This is a very ancient drink originating in the north of Europe. To some new honey, strained, add spring water; put a whole egg into it; boil this liquor till the egg swims above the liquor; strain, pour in a cask. To every fifteen gallons add two ounces of white Jamaica ginger, bruised, one ounce of cloves and mace, one and a half ounces of cinnamon, all bruised together, and tied up in a muslin bag; quicken the fermentation with yeast; when worked sufficiently, bung up; in six weeks draw off into bottles.

Honey Wine Made from Combs: Boil the combs from which the honey has been drained with sufficient water to make a tolerably sweet liquor; ferment with yeast and proceed as above. Another method is to add a handful of hops and sufficient brandy to the comb liquor.

Dandelion Wine

Put one full quart of dandelion blooms, 1 gallon water, 1 lemon cut in slices (not peeled) 2½ pounds of sugar in a kettle and boil 5 minutes, then pour into a jar; when cold, add 2 tablespoonfuls of good yeast. Keep in a warm place 3 days until it ferments, then strain and bottle; cork tightly.

Orange Wine

Wipe the oranges with a wet cloth, peel off the yellow rind very thin, squeeze the oranges and strain the juice through a hair sieve; measure the juice after it is strained, and for each gallon allow three pounds of granulated sugar, the white and shell of the egg (crushed fine) and the water over the fire, and stir them every two minutes until the egg begins to harden; then boil the syrup until it looks clear under the froth of the egg which will form on the surface, strain the syrup, pour it upon the orange rind, and let it stand over night, strain the second day, add the orange-juice and again let it stand over night, strain the second day and put it into a tight cask with a small cake of yeast to about ten gallons of wine and leave the bung out of the cask until the wine ceases to ferment; the hissing sound continues as long as fermentation is in progress. When fermentation ceases, close the cask by driving in the bung and let the wine stand nine months before bottling it. Three months after it is bottled it can be used. A glass of brandy added to each gallon of wine after fermentation ceases will improve the wine. This fine wine can be made at very little expense if oranges are purchased by the box during the most plentiful season of the year.

An engraving of an old stationary cider press used to produce apple juice, cider and vinegar. Fresh cider was heartily enjoyed as a beverage and vinegar was important to the preservation of garden vegetables. *Courtesy of the Seattle Historical Society*

BUTTER, CHEESE, EGGS

Clarified Butter

Put ½ pound fresh butter in pan, stand over a very little heat, boil very gently, skimming well, until it looks like a clear salad oil, pour very carefully into a sauce-boat, keeping back the sediment. Serve with boiled fish, artichokes, asparagus, etc.

Freshening Butter

Melt the butter and skim it. Then put into it a piece of toast free from burn. In a few minutes it will lose its offensive taste and smell, which the toast has absorbed.

Storing Butter

Into six pounds of fresh butter work a large spoonful of salt and a tablespoonful each of saltpeter and powdered white sugar. Pack in a crock that is perfectly clean and cover with salt.

Butter Substitute

In a glass jar put 6 level tablespoons of fresh melted beef fat, 6 level tablespoons of sweet milk, 1 teaspoon salt, 1 drop yellow coloring, and shake until hard ball is formed.

Cottage Cheese

Put a pan of thick milk on the stove where it is not too hot, let it scald until whey rises to the top. Do not let it boil or the curd will be tough. Drain through a colander, put in a deep dish, add a teaspoon of salt and enough cream, sweet or sour, to make the cheese the consistency of putty and serve.

Dutch Cheese

Put two quarts of dairy sour milk in a flat pan and set on a back of a wood burning stove so milk will barely keep warm. When milk turns to curds, skim off the whey, then drain in a clean cloth until curds are perfectly dry. Add cream and salt to taste.

Curd Cheese

Put 1 quart milk in a basin, add strained juice of 3 lemons to it, and let it stand in a temperature of 54° for 12 hours. Have ready a muslin about 18 inches square, put it over a basin and pour the curd into this, tie it round with string, and hang on a nail over a sink to drain for a few hours. Then put between two plates, with a weight on top, and press till all the moisture is pressed out. Turn out, and eat like ordinary cheese, or with sugar or fresh fruit.

Artificial Goat's Milk

Chop 1 oz. of suet very finely, tie loosely in a muslin bag, and boil slowly in a quart of new milk for ½ hour. Sweeten with white sugar, or any nice syrup that is palatable. Very good in wasting diseases, and a good substitute for cod-liver oil in many cases.

The Nonpareil Butter Worker.

Courtesy of the Seattle Historical Society

Preserving Eggs

Pour three pails of water over four quarts of unslacked lime and when it is cold add one-half pound of salt and one ounce of cream of tartar. Eggs covered with this liquid will keep a long time.

Preserving Eggs

Be sure they are fresh. If possible have them rubbed over with butter whenever laid. Place them points down in a stone jar and pour over them the following brine, which is enough for 150:—1 pint slacked lime, 1 pint salt, 2 oz. cream of tartar, and 4 gallons water. Boil all together 10 minutes. Skim and when cold pour over the eggs carefully. They can also be kept in salt, tightly packed but not touching. If buttered the day they are laid (to close the pores of the egg) they may be merely placed in egg-boxed and tied up, or put into racks for the purpose. They must be kept on end.

Testing Eggs

If the end of a fresh egg be applied to the tongue, it feels cold; that of a stale egg feels warm. This is due to the white of a fresh egg being in contact with the shell, and abstracting the heat from the tongue more rapidly then does the air-bubble in the stale one. Fresh eggs are more transparent in the centre, stale ones at the end.

Forcemeat

Boil 4 eggs hard; take out yolks and mash them with the butter, adding ½ oz. parsley, ½ oz. beetroot, ¼ oz. sweet leeks, ¼ oz. sweet marjoram, Winter savoury and lemon thyme mixed, and ½ pound bread crumbs; season with pepper and salt and a little nutmeg. Add 3 tablespoonfuls cream and 2 eggs (well beaten); melt some butter in tin and put in forcemeat and roast before fire in Dutch oven. Serve with brown sauce, part of which may be poured on dish, and garnish with whites of eggs cut small.

Mayonnaise

Put the yolk of 1 egg (raw) in a basin; add ¼ teaspoonful mustard, pepper, salt and cayenne; then ½ pint salad oil, drop by drop, stirring quickly all the time; then 1 dessertspoonful vinegar, and a few drops lemon juice. The sauce must be kept quite stiff. Should sauce curdle, drop in another yolk of egg and it will be brought to its original state.

Salad Dressing

Beat the yolks of two newly laid eggs well with a little mustard, pepper and salt; then gradually mix ½ pint salad oil, and, when well mixed, add tarragon vinegar and two good teaspoonfuls of castor sugar.

Road house thirty miles from Dawson run by the Killoen Family. Sociability and neighborliness of those early times were characteristic of the West. Transportation was difficult; neighbors were few and far between. Social visits and necessary traveling stops were enjoyed to the fullest extent. *Courtesy of the Seattle Historical Society*

POULTRY AND PORK.

Courtesy of the Seattle Historical Society

SWEETS

Candy

In making all candies, except those that scorch easily, as soon as the sugar is dissolved and it begins to boil it is well to cover the vessel for a short time, say two or three minutes, that the steam may soften any sugar sticking to the sides of the kettle, then to take a damp cloth and carefully remove all undissolved sugar. This is important that the candy may not "grain" or turn back to sugar. If the candy is one that easily burns and requires stirring the kettle must be cleaned without steaming.

Also to prevent sugaring pure glucose or cream of tartar can be used. Vinegar can be substituted but it is not as good. Be sure there is no sugar on the platter or marble upon which the candy is poured. Needlessly stirring or handling the batch while cooling will sometimes cause "graining." If in spite of all precautions this happens, cover with water, again place on the stove and re-cook, but it will seldom be as nice as when cooked but once.

Colouring For Fancy Jellies, Creams, Etc.

Ornamental sweets should not be obtained at the risk of health. Simple vegetable colouring should only be permitted. The following can be safely recommended:

Red: It is usual for cooks to boil 15 grains of cochineal in the finest powder, with 1½ drachms of cream of tartar in ½ pint of water very slowly for ½ hour, adding piece of alum as large as a pea. The cochineal insect may be used in safety in such a small quantity; but we would rather recommend the juice of beetroot drawn out over the fire in a little water, with the addition of a squeeze of lemon juice.

Green: A beautiful colour may be obtained from the expressed juice of spinach leaves.

Yellow: If a transparent colour be required, orange or lemon jelly dissolved; if opaque, the pounded yolks of eggs.

White: Pounded almonds or arrowroot.

Table for Testing Candy

Smooth (218 degrees): The boiling syrup or candy can just be detected when dropped into water and it about the consistency of molasses. Used for crystallizing creams, candies, etc.

Thread (235 degrees): The candy will stick or cling to the finger but will not retain the shape of a ball when rolled between them. (Use for making liquors, etc.)

Soft ball or feather (240 degrees): The candy when cooled in water and rolled between the fingers will take the form of a soft ball. (Used for fondants, cream goods and fruit candies.)

Hard ball (245 to 250 degrees): When cooled in water and rolled between the fingers the candy will take the form of a rather hard ball but it is not hard enough to crack when bent or broken. (Used for some fondants and cream goods.)

First crack (250 degrees): Will just crack when bent or broken between the fingers. (Used for caramels, butter scotch, Japanese cocoanut bars, etc.)

Second crack (255 degrees): Will crack more easily than for first crack and will chew free without sticking to the teeth. (Used for most taffies or candies that are pulled.)

Dry crack (300 to 310 degrees): When cooled in water it will break brittle like glass in the fingers. If cooked much longer the candy will color and burn. (Used for stick candy and all kinds of hard clear candies.)

Candied Fruit

Make a syrup with 1 pound sugar and ½ teacupful water. When boiling put in any preserved fruit and stir gently till they are crystallized. Lift out, and dry in oven, but don't let them get coloured.

Peanut Brittle

Sprinkle 1 cup shelled peanuts with salt in buttered pan. Heat 1 cup sugar in granite pan. Keep stirring constantly till melted. Pour over nuts.

Peanut Brittle

Put one cup of sugar into a frying pan and shake briskly over the fire until the sugar is melted. Then add a cup of chopped peanuts. Take care not to burn the peanuts.

Cinnamon Drops

Mix ½ oz. powdered cinnamon, or ½ teaspoonful oil of cinnamon, with 1 pound pounded sugar and ½ pint water. Boil the syrup till it snaps when put in cold water in about ¼ hour. Then spread it on a large flat dish, well oiled, and score, before it hardens, into small squares, or drop it evenly on paper.

Cracker Jack

Take two cups of sugar, one cup of molasses and two tablespoonfuls of vinegar. Boil until it cracks when tested in cold water. Then take from the fire, add one-half teaspoonful of soda, beat briskly and pour over pop-corn and chopped peanuts.

Chewing Taffy

For two cups of sugar take one cup of water, when it is boiling add two tablespoonfuls of vinegar and a piece of butter the size of a walnut, let cook until it will harden in water, add the flavoring and remove from the stove. Pull when it is cool enough.

Molasses Taffy

Two cups of sugar, one cup of molasses, one teaspoon of soda and one tablespoonful of vinegar; boil until brittle and pull.

Toffee

Boil briskly for 2 minutes 6 pounds brown sugar in brass pan with 1 pint cold water, add ½ pound fresh butter and boil 10 minutes longer; when it should be brittle. Try with cold water, then pour on buttered dish, and when half cold mark into diamonds with oiled knife.

A picnic at Cedar Home Farm on September 3, 1899. *Courtesy of the Seattle Historical Society*

A scene showing the interior of an early sawmill or lumber camp kitchen. *Courtesy of the Seattle Historical Society*

Candy Cough Drops

Take two and one-half pounds of granulated sugar, one-fourth teaspoonful of cream tartar and enough water to dissolve. Cook to the dry crack of until it will break like glass when tested in cold water. After testing place a little in the mouth and if it will not stick to the teeth when chewed it is ready to take from the stove and pour upon greased marble or platter. When on platter add one-half ounce powdered willow charcoal and one-fourth tablespoonful of oil of anise, fold and kneed thoroughly while as hot as can be handled. Then cut into small pieces or drops with shears. The batch must be handled rapidly or it will cool and harden before cut into convenient pieces. These are some of the best cough drops made and will last a long time.

Brown Betty

Soak old or hard bread and line baking dish with these crumbs. Then put in a layer of apples sliced very thin over which sprinkle sugar and add little bits of butter; make alternate layers of crumbs and apples till dish is full, having the last layer of crumbs. Sprinkle this well with sugar and bits of butter and cinnamon; add ½ cup water and bake half an hour. To be eaten with sweetened cream.

Christmas Cakes

Take equal weight of chopped apples and raisins, brown sugar, candied peel and currants. To 1 pound of mixture put juice and rind of lemon and ½ teaspoonful mixed spice. Make into small cakes with flaky pastry, brush over with white of egg and sprinkle sugar over.

Apple or Fruit Cups

Sift together one pint of flour, a half teaspoonful of salt, two tablespoonfuls of sugar and one teaspoonful of baking powder. Beat one egg, add four tablespoonfuls of milk and stir into the dry mixture, adding more milk as necessary to make a thick batter. Add two tablespoonfuls of melted butter and beat hard. Butter some baking cups and put in each a spoonful of the batter. Add a quarter of a tart apple, and more batter to cover and two-thirds fill the cup. Steam or bake and serve with hard sauce. Any kind of fresh fruit may be used instead of the apple.

Apple Dicky

A lump of butter the size of an egg, 1 cup of sugar, 2 cups of flour, 3 teaspoonfuls of baking powder, ½ cup of water, 1 egg, a pinch of salt; put sliced apples in a baking dish, pour the batter over them and bake.

Apple Dumplings

One tablespoonful melted butter, one tablespoon sugar, one-half cup milk, one teaspoonful baking powder, flour to the consistency of layer cake; butter a baking dish well-filled with sliced apples and turn this batter over and bake a few minutes. Serve with cream and sugar.

Marzipan

Mix 1 pound sifted loaf sugar and 1 pound ground almonds, then add, little by little, 2 fresh stiff egg whites, and few drops essence almonds until mixture assumes appearance of paste. As some eggs contain more white than others, a little less than the 2 may be enough. Paste must be quite firm. Form into blocks, and dry very slowly in a moderate oven.

Johnny Cake

Put 2 breakfast-cupfuls four, 1 teacupful sugar, and 2 teaspoonfuls baking-powder in basin. Mix well, rub in piece of butter size of a walnut, add 1 teacupful any fruit liked, such as sultanas, or currants, or peel or preserved ginger, or grated cocoanut, 1 egg (well beaten) and a cupful milk. Pour into greased tin and bake about 1 hour.

Johnny Cake

"Two cups Indian, one cup wheat,
One cup sour milk, one cup sweet,
One cup good eggs that you can eat,
One-half cup molasses, too,
One-half cup sugar add thereto,
Salt and soda, each a spoon,
Mix up quickly and bake it soon."

Pork Cake

One pound fat pork, 1 pound seeded raisins, 1 pound dates, 1 pound currants, 1 pound figs, 1 teaspoonful soda, 8 cups flour, 1 pint of hot water poured over the flour and let cool. Mix all together and bake.

Almond Paste

Mix 1 pound almonds and 1 pound castor sugar, add 1 tablespoonful orange-flower water, and 8 or 9 drops essence almonds, then beat 2 eggs and knead them into the almonds, spread on top of cake and smooth with clean knife.

Almond Dust

This is made by pounding any quantity of blanched sweet almonds which have been thoroughly browned in a moderate oven. Use for garnishing cakes and sweet dishes.

Ratafia Icing

Whites of 4 eggs to ½ pound icing sugar and ½ pound ground almonds. Whip eggs to stiff froth; add teaspoonful essence almonds. May either make cake or icing. If for icing, papercake, spread, and just brown in moderate oven. Add more white of egg if for macaroons and sweeten to taste.

Bachelor's Buttons

Rub 4 oz. butter into 10 oz. flour; 2 oz. of sugar; beat 2 eggs; add to the mixture. Break off pieces size of a nut, sprinkle sugar over, and bake on buttered paper a light brown.

Gingerbread Snaps

Rub 3 pound flour and 1½ pound butter, together, add 1 pound sugar, 3½ pound treacle, 2 oz. ginger, 1 oz. each of allspice, candied peel and lemon peel, 1 nutmeg and make into paste. Lay them on tins size of a nut.

Merry Christmas!
A festive dinner at the William Ragless place on December 25, 1916. *Courtesy of the Washington State University, Henderson Collection*

Rolled Oat Cookies

Cream 1 cup butter, 1 cup sugar. Add 2 eggs and 1 teaspoon soda dissolved in 2 teaspoons hot water. Mix 2 cups flour, 3 cups Rolled Oats, in with the eggs and shortening and 1 teaspoon vanilla. Work with hands. Drop on greased pan and bake. Have the taste of cocoanut.

Dough Nuts

Put into a basin ½ pound of flour, a good teaspoon of baking-powder, a pinch of salt; mix these well together with the tips of fingers, add 1 tablespoon of sugar, and rub in a piece of butter the size of a walnut. Make a well in the centre, drop in one egg, and moisten with enough buttermilk to make a stiff dough. Drop a teaspoonful of the mixture into boiling fat, and cook from 5 to 6 minutes until a nice brown colour. Take out and drain on paper; dust over with fine sugar. A few drops of flavouring essence may be added.

Coffee Kringles

2 oz. butter in cup, melted gradually over boiling water. Break 4 yolks of eggs in basin with 1 white, beat up and fork well. Add to eggs 2 oz. white sugar, also the melted butter. Stir with wooden spoon till quite smooth. Then add all at once ½ pound flour. Mix all to stiff paste. Flour board and knead paste well together. Roll out ½ inch thickness. Cut in shapes. Prick with fork dipped in flour. Bake for 10 to 15 minutes. If liked brown, egg over.

Scotch Scones

Sift together 1 quart of flour, ½ teaspoonful of salt, 1 teaspoonful of sugar and 2 heaping teaspoonfuls of baking powder; rub in 1 large tablespoonful of butter, cold; add 2 beaten eggs and nearly ½ pint of sweet milk; mix into smooth dough; knead quickly and roll out to ⅓ of an inch in thickness; cut out with knife into squares about the size of soda crackers; fold each corner-wise, to form triangles; place in pan and brush over with egg and milk; bake 10 minutes in hot oven.

With more cooks than men to feed, the lucky diner can have ample servings of the main dish and pie to follow. In the background kitchen utensils can be seen hanging on the wall. A 'cook shack' scene on the Odegard dryland farm in July of 1912.
Courtesy of Washington State University, Henderson Collection

Scones

Mix 4 teacupfuls flour, 1 teaspoonful bicarbonate of soda, 1½ do. cream of tartar, ½ do. salt, 2 do. sugar or 2 do. syrup (which makes the scones a light brown colour). Rub into the flour a dessertspoonful of butter. Mix well, and then add buttermilk to make a soft dough. Care must be taken to mix it thoroughly, until all the flour is absorbed, and it is firm enough to handle without working it after it is on the bake-board. Sprinkle flour on board, then put out half the dough; sprinkle a little flour on the top, then gently work with fingers into a round half-inch thick. Cut in four and fire on a moderately heated gridle. The above mixture makes 8 scones, and they are delicious if the above rules are observed. The secret of having nice scones is not to touch the dough after it is on the board, except to work it out as directed. By putting 1 teacupful of oatmeal to 3 teacupfuls of flour, with the same mixture as for white scones, you have a nice short scone.

Cracker Custard

Soak four crackers in one pint of milk, add the yolks of three eggs, three tablespoonfuls sugar. Bake as a custard. When cooked put any kind of jelly or canned fruit over it, then put on the white of the eggs beaten stiff and bake until brown. Serve with cream.

Corn Pudding

One pint grated corn, 1 pint of milk or, if canned corn is used, then less milk, 1 tablespoon of flour wet with milk, a pinch of salt, 2 tablespoonfuls sugar, 2 eggs, a few bits of butter on top. Bake about an hour in a slow oven. Stir when beginning to brown.

Date Pudding

Chop ¼ pound suet finely, stone and cut up 1 pound dates, ¼ pound brown sugar, ¼ nutmeg grated, mix all well together, using as little water to moisten as possible. Boil in buttered basin 4 hours.

Baked or Boiled Carrot Pudding (1861)

Ingredients:

½ lb. bread crumbs	4 oz. suet
¼ stoned raisins	¾ lb. carrots
¼ lb. currants	3 oz. sugar
3 oz. milk	¼ tsp. nutmeg

Made:

Boil the carrots until tender enough to mash to a pulp; add the remaining ingredients, and moisten with sufficient milk to make the pudding of the consistency of thick batter. If to be boiled, put the mixture into a buttered basin, tie it down with a cloth and boil for 2½ hours; if to be baked, put it into a pie-dish, and bake for nearly an hour; turn it out of the dish, strew sifted sugar over it and serve.

Time:

2½ hours to boil
1 hour to bake
Average cost 1s. 2d.
Sufficient for 5 or 6 persons.

Fannie Farmer's Pudding

½ cup cornstarch	1 teaspoon vanilla
¼ cup sugar	3 egg whites
4½ cups milk	

In a small mixing bowl stir together the cornstarch, sugar and salt; gradually stir in ½ cup of the milk, keeping smooth. In a medium saucepan over moderately low heat, scald the remaining milk—tiny bubbles will appear around the edge; stir in the cornstarch mixture; stirring constantly, bring to a boil and boil 3 minutes; remove from heat. Stir in vanilla. Should not be cooled longer than it takes to beat the egg whites. Pour into a 5 cup mold. Cover with plastic wrap. Chill until set—about 3 hours. Run a small metal spatula round edge (and if a tube mold is used, around tube), invert and turn out—pudding will flatten slightly. Serve with sliced sweetened strawberries or peaches. Makes 6 to 8 servings.

Note: Be sure to keep the heat lower than medium during the cooking to insure the mixture thickening smoothly and evenly. The pudding will not look entirely combined when the egg whites are folded in, but it will be completely smooth when it is ready to serve.

Cottage Pudding

One cup milk, 1 cup sugar, 1 egg, lump of butter the size of an egg, 1 pint of flour, a pinch of salt, 1 heaping teaspoonful baking powder. Sauce: One egg, 1 cup sugar, 1 teaspoonful flour, small piece of butter; mix and add boiling water; let come to boil; flavor with vanilla.

Humble Pudding

Mix 2 pounds potatoes mashed, 1 pint milk, 2 eggs well beaten, 2 oz. sugar and a pinch salt thoroughly and bake ¾ hour.

Indian Pudding

Stir 6 tablespoonfuls of cornmeal into 1 quart of scalded milk, let it cool just a little. Set aside to cool, then add ½ cup of sugar, 2 eggs well beaten, ½ teaspoonful of salt, 1 tablespoonful butter, dust of cinnamon. Bake slowly one hour. Sauce: Stir to a cream a full cup of sugar and scant ½ cup of butter and juice of one lemon.

Steamed Pudding

To make steamed pudding use 1 cup of chopped suet, 1 cup each of raisins, currants and chopped apples, 1 cup of New Orleans molasses, 1 cup of sour milk (can use sweet), ½ teaspoon salt and 1 teaspoon soda. Stir a trifle thicker than for cake. Steam for three hours with a steamer tightly covered.

Tipsy Pudding

One of the choice recipes of our yesterday's era. It appeared in the place of honor on New Year's Day. The secret for a successful outcome is to use a very stale, very porous cake. A broken, not cut, sunshine cake at least four days old, should be soaked in sherry. Allow about one cup sherry to a quarter of a good sized cake. An hour later cover the cake with a soft custard flavored with rum. Serve very cold.

Elderberry Pie

Five tablespoonfuls elderberries, 3 tablespoonfuls sugar, 5 tablespoonfuls molasses, 2 tablespoonfuls cider vinegar, 1 tablespoonful flour sprinkled on top. Bake in 2 crusts.

Shoo-Fly Pie

Make regular pie crust and fill as follows: 2 cups boiling water, 1 cup syrup and 2 teaspoonfuls baking soda and crumbs; pour the boiling water over the syrup and add the soda. Directions for making the crumbs: One cup of lard, 3 cups of flour, 1½ cups of sugar; same to be used in place of the top crust.

Plain Pastry

Have all materials cold, including the bowl in which the pastry is to be mixed. Measure 2 cups pastry flour, ½ teaspoonful, and 1 teaspoonful sugar into the flour sifter and sift into the bowl. Measure ¼ cup lard and ¼ cup butter and with the pastry cutter or knife cut this well into the flour. Do not put the hands into it, as the main thing in pastry is to keep it cold and it is the expansion of this cold air in the oven when baking that makes the pastry light and flaky. Add cold water a little at a time and as mixed push to one side; add more and do the same, until water has been added sufficient to take up the dryness and no more. Now bring all together in one mass, cover and set in a cold place two or three hours, if possible, as the crust is then much easier to handle and more flaky when baked. This recipe will answer for all pies.

Empanadas With Vanilla Sauce

1½ cups finely chopped beef
1 pound jar mincemeat
2 ounces suet, chopped finely
1½ teaspoons crushed Oregano
¼ cup sugar
1 tablespoon grated lemon peel
1 recipe plain pastry (using 2 cups flour)

Combine beef, mincemeat, suet, Oregano, sugar, and lemon peel. Roll pastry and cut in 6 inch circles. Place ⅓ cup filling on each pastry circle; fold in half, and flute edge. Prick to allow steam to escape. Fry in deep hot fat. Serve with hot vanilla sauce. Yield: 12 turnovers.

Vanilla Sauce:

¾ cup butter
3 tablespoons cornstarch
3 cups boiling water
3 teaspoons vanilla
1½ cups sugar

Melt butter; blend in cornstarch and sugar. Add boiling water, stirring constantly, and cook until thickened. Add vanilla just before serving. Vanilla pods have a much better flavour than the essence. Stir the pod among the substance to be flavoured till it has enough, then wash pod in two or three waters, and dry for future use. Will last a long time.

Marketing day at Quincy, Washington in 1911. *Courtesy of the Washington State University Library, Henderson Collection*

Learning to garden was part of almost every boy's and girl's education. Pictured is an old-fashioned gardening class at Rose School in Seattle, Washington. *Courtesy of the Seattle Historical Society*

VEGETABLES

Gather vegetables in cool of morning. If the sun is on them the vegetables will be tough and discoloured. Green vegetables should be crisp, fresh-coloured and sweet-smelling, and root vegetables firm. Keep in cool, dark, draughty place such as the floor of a cellar. Be careful they do not touch one another. Cover celery and cauliflower from the light with paper. Before washing vegetables, give them a little slap against the palm of the hand, and much of the dirt, sand and insects will drop off, which would otherwise stick when plunged into the water. Soak cabbage and cauliflower in cold water, with a tablespoonful vinegar added. Better than salt; salt only kills the caterpillars—vinegar also draws them out. The water should not boil before wanted, or vegetables will be discoloured. All green vegetables float on the water first, and when cooked fall to the bottom. To prevent vegetables from smelling the house when boiling, put a piece of bread in muslin and put in pan. A little vinegar may be kept boiling on the stove while onions or cabbage is being cooked; this also will prevent the disagreeable odour going through the house. The proportion of salt to allow in cooking vegetables is one teaspoonful to every half-gallon of water. Remember that all green vegetables, except spinach, are cooked with the cover of the saucepan off. Vegetables of strong flavour, which include most green vegetables, should be well covered with fast-boiling water and cooked rather rapidly till done, but if at any time the water goes off the boil replace the lid till water boils up again, as slow boiling spoils the colour of all green vegetables. A good rule is that vegetables which grow below the ground should always be put in cold water for cooking, while all that grow above should be plunged in boiling water. All white vegetables need a little acid; all green a little soda. When boiling green vegetables of any kind, if a piece of dripping about the size of a walnut is put in the centre of the vegetables just as they begin to boil it will prevent all boiling over. After cooking, vegetables must be well drained of all superfluous moisture whether they are to be served with sauce over or not. Before cooking onions, let them lie, when peeled, in a little boiling water with a tiny piece of soda added.

When preparing onions for cooking it will be found much more comfortable work if they are peeled or sliced under water. Hold in the lap a large bowl filled with clear water, and work with the hands under the water. Onions done in this manner will not cause tears or stained fingers. To clean a knife that has been used for cutting onions, hold it under the cold-water tap. It is a mistake to use hot water to remove the smell of onions from a knife. Onions should not be eaten after they have lain about peeled and cut, as they absorb any bad odour or infectious condition that may exist. All waste leaves of vegetables should be burned; if thrown into the dust-bin they will decay, and help to create bad smells and fever. When burning vegetable refuse in stove or fireplace, put a handful of salt into the fire with it, and there will be no unpleasant odour. Tomatoes get soft if soaked in water. Many varieties of beans become tough when moistened. Most fruits are made mouldy by soaking, and beetroots keep fresh for a long time without water. Lettuce, endive, spinach, asparagus, etc. are all the better for the addition of water.

To Keep Vegetables

If vegetables are to be kept a long time they should be pulled on a dry day and the tops should be cut off and trimmed. Pack them in layers in barrels or boxes with moss between and over them. The moss keeps them from shriveling and yet keeps out any excess of moisture.

Vegetables should be kept at as low a temperature as possible without freezing. Apples will stand a very low temperature but sweet potatoes should have a dry and warm atmosphere and should be kept well packed with dry leaves. Squashes should be kept in a dry place and as cool as possible without freezing.

Parsnips and Salsify

Unless the climate is very severe they should be left in the ground all winter, otherwise they should be buried in a deep pit in the garden.

Cabbages

Cut them off near the head and carry to cellar with leaves on, break off the leaves and pack the cabbages in a tight box with the stems upward. When the box is nearly full cover with loose leaves and put the lid on to keep rats out. They should be kept in a dry cellar.

Onions

The best way is to spread them over the floor.

Parsley Green and Fresh

Make a strong, boiling hot pickle of salt and water and keep it in this for use. If wanted for soups and stuffing, hang it up in bunches in a dry attic, with the blossoms down.

Potatoes

They should be kept in a cool, dark place. When old and likely to sprout, put them into a basket and lower them for a minute or two into boiling water. Let them dry and put in sacks. This destroys the germs without injuring the potato and allows it to keep its flavor until late.

Turnips

Bury them deep in the ground and they will keep until spring.

Yankee Clipper Beans

2 cups navy beans	½ teaspoon dry mustard
¼ pound fat salt pork, sliced	2 tablespoons molasses
	1 small onion, quartered
½ teaspoon salt	¼ cup brown sugar

Wash beans, cover with water and soak overnight. Cook slowly until skins burst or until just tender. Drain, reserving liquor. Place half the beans in bean pot or casserole. Bury part of pork in beans and add half of combined remaining ingredients. Add remaining beans and seasonings. Place remaining salt pork over top. Cover with bean liquor. Cover and bake in slow oven (250 degrees—300 degrees F.) 6 to 8 hours, if necessary add more liquid.

Boston Baked Beans

Wash one quart of small white beans and soak them over night in soft water. In the morning drain and put with them 1 pound of fresh pork and boil until the beans begin to split open. Put them in a colander and rinse with cold water; then put about half of them in an earthen pot, lay in the pork, cover with the remainder of the beans. Mix 1 tablespoonful of molasses and 1 teaspoonful of mustard with a teacup of water and pour over the beans, adding enough boiling water to cover. Bake 4 hours, adding water occasionally.

Fried Beets

Cook as for beet pickles. Pare and cut into cubes or slices, as preferred. Heat some butter, pepper and salt in a skillet, add the beets and fry slowly until ready to serve.

Escalloped Corn

Butter baking tin, put layer of corn then buttered crumbs until ¾ full seasoning each layer well. Add milk until quite moist. Have buttered crumbs on top. Bake until brown or about 30 to 45 minutes.

Dandelion Greens

2 pounds dandelion greens	1 tablespoon butter
	Salt and pepper

Dandelions should be used before they blossom, as they become bitter after that time. Cut off the roots, pick the greens over carefully, and wash them well in several waters. Place them in a kettle, add a little boiling water, and boil until tender. Salt the water just before cooking is completed. When done, lift them into a colander, press them to drain off all the water, and chop. Add butter, salt and pepper.

Dandelion Dish

Take a sharp knife and cut dandelions at root, clean them carefully, put in chopping bowl and chop up fine. Heat in skillet one-half cup of meat drippings, one-third cup vinegar, salt and pepper to taste, pour over dandelions and add four hard boiled eggs, stir all together and serve immediately.

The Northrup's old log house at Lake Union in 1889-90. Modern cooks would be hard put to rival the dishes that were produced from produce on hand. There was beef and wild game; vegetable planting was among the first chores. There were wild berries such as huckleberries, elderberries, sarvis and choke cherries. *Courtesy of the Seattle Historical Society*

Beetroot

Wash and brush the roots, being careful to avoid breaking off the fibres, to prevent the juice escaping, and spoiling the colour and flavour. Put them in a pan of boiling water; adding salt and a small piece of soda, and boil from 1 to 2 hours, according to size. Put into cold water, and rub off the skin with the hand. Slice them, and serve either with vinegar or mustard sauce. Beetroot is very good boiled as usual, and served covered with white or parsley sauce, or with Spanish onions sliced.

When a piece of straw will pierce the beets, they are ready.

Kale or Curly Greens

Strip leaves from stalks of 1 pound fresh kale and wash thoroughly. Place in 2 quarts of boiling water, and boil rapidly 25 minutes, or rather less if very fresh and young, but much longer if old. Drain well, pressing all water out with a plate.

Leeks

Trim off root and outer skin of 8 to 10 medium-sized leeks, wasting as little as possible; cut off top leafy part, so that all are one length. Throw in boiling salted water and boil rapidly ½ hour. If very young, rather less time; if full-grown, rather more. Drain well, and serve on toast with melted butter over. If leeks are very small, tie in a bunch before putting to boil.

Egg Plant

Pare the egg plant and slice it thin; sprinkle each slice with salt; lay slice upon slice and place a plate upon the top. The salt will drain out the disagreeable, bitter flavor. Half an hour before serving wipe each slice dry, dip into beaten egg, then in fine cracker crumbs and fry in plenty of hot butter; drain on a brown wrapping paper as they come from the frying pan, crisp and brown. Serve at once on a hot platter.

Crunchy Corn Fritters

A way to use corn cut from cooked leftover cobs is in fritters made with cornmeal. These corn fritters have crunchy exteriors and soft insides. Serve with maple syrup or with fried chicken, bacon, ham or pork sausage.

½ cup flour, stir to aerate before measuring
1 teaspoon baking powder
¼ teaspoon salt
¼ cup enriched yellow cornmeal
¼ cup milk
1 tablespoon butter or margarine (melted) or vegetable oil
1 cup corn kernels, cut from leftover cobs
1 egg

In a medium mixing bowl thoroughly stir together the flour, baking powder and salt; stir in cornmeal.

In a small mixing bowl beat together the egg and milk until combined; add to cornmeal mixture with the butter and corn; stir just until dry ingredients are moistened.

Drop by generous tablespoons into hot deep fat (360 degrees) without crowding and fry until browned, turning once—about 3 minutes in all. Drain on absorbent paper. Serve hot with maple syrup.

Makes 4 to 6 servings.

Jerusalem Artichokes

1 pound artichokes, well washed and scraped, each one thrown into fresh cold water and vinegar; when all are done, rinse in water and put into boiling milk and water, and salt. Boil quickly with lid off, pierce with fork to know if done. Lift out carefully on to dish directly (if left in milk and water they turn black, or if any eyes were left in), and cover with sauce. Sauce—1 oz. butter, 1 oz. flour, 1 yolk egg, lemon juice, salt, pepper, 3 gills milk, and 1 tablespoonful cream. Melt butter, add flour. Stir, cook a few minutes, add milk gradually and cook a little. Beat egg and cream, and add, after sauce is off boil, lemon juice last, and seasoning. Pour over, and add minced parsley if liked.

Lentil Cutlets

Soak 1 pound lentils overnight; put them in a saucepan, with sufficient water to cover them, and stew gently till tender. Boil 1 beetroot whole, and cut it in small pieces; chop 1 large onion and fry it. Then mix 1 tablespoon chopped parsley, 1 teaspoon thyme, ½ teacup ketchup, 1 oz. butter pepper and salt, and put them aside until quite cool; then mould into shapes the size of a cutlet; brush them with 2 beaten eggs; dip them in fine bread crumbs and fry in boiling oil.

The windmill was a sentinel on homestead farms in the early 20th Century. Silhouetted against the sky, it seems to guard the family and friends who have gathered to pick ripe corn on the Schmoe Ranch. *Courtesy of the Henderson Collection, Washington State University*

Workers in Mr. J. E. Overbay's cabbage patch on August 8, 1915. *Courtesy of the Henderson Collection, Washington State University Library*

Potato Birdies

Take a few boiled potatoes and form into scones. Have some mincemeat ready; spread meat pretty dry over half of scone and turn over other half on meat and pinch all rand. Fried in boiling fat and served hot, these make tasty tit-bits for either breakfast or supper.

German Potato Pancakes

3 to 4 cups grated potatoes
3 egg yolks
1 cup flour
1 teaspoon baking powder
1 onion grated

Mix well and fold in stiffly beaten egg whites, and fry in pan of deep fat. Sauce—1 cup raisins, 1 cup vinegar, 2 cups water, 3 cups sugar. Boil and add thickening made of flour and water to desired thickness.

Baked Sauer Kraut

Put one quart of sauer kraut in a granite kettle with one pound of fresh pork, cover with cold water. Place in a moderate oven and bake two hours. Serve hot.

Mock Oyster Soup

Scrape 12 stalks vegetables oysters and throw at once into cold water with 1 tablespoonful vinegar or lemon juice to prevent discoloring; cut thin slices; put these into the stew pan with 1 quart boiling water, 1 slice onion and 1 sprig of parsley; cook slowly thirty minutes or until tender. Put 1 pint milk into the double boiler; add 1 tablespoonful butter and 1 tablespoonful flour rubbed together, stir until it is smooth and begins to thicken. When the vegetable oyster is done rub through the colander and pour into the double boiler, season with salt and pepper and serve.

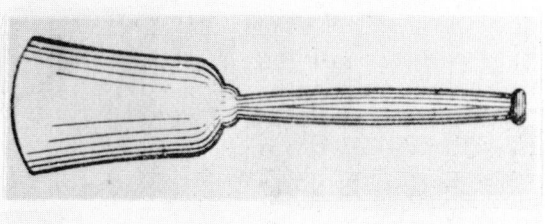

Wooden Vegetable Masher
A wooden vegetable masher is indispensable when making jellies and purees.

Stewed Lettuce

Using 6 or 7 lettuces, trim away all outer leaves and stalks (which are bitter), wash carefully and boil in plenty water for 20 to 30 minutes. Drain and press well. Chop lightly. Put in clean pan with 1 oz. butter and 1 tablespoonful lemon juice and toss till quite hot. Serve with croutons of toast.

Green Salad

Chop finely 2 or 3 spring onions, shred some quite fresh lettuces with the fingers, add 2 tablespoonfuls pure olive oil and juice of ½ lemon. Mix well together, garnish with fresh mustard and cress and radishes. To wash mustard and cress, put in large basin of cold water and shake well. Lift out carefully. If necessary rinse in fresh water. Lift the cress from the water, place in a clean dry cloth, gather the corners together and swing till all moisture is out. Shake mustard and cress apart and it is ready.

Nut Cutlets

Rub 4 oz. nuts, any kind (pine kernels good, or hazel) and 2 oz. vermicelli through nut-mill and mix with a dash of tomato sauce, a dash of any other good sauce to a stiff consistency. Roll out this paste ¼ inch thick and cut in cutlet shape. Brush over with egg, roll in bread crumbs and fry.

Nut Loaf

One cup rolled crackers, 1 cup chopped English walnuts, beaten yolks of 2 eggs, season with pepper and salt, 2 teaspoonfuls sugar, stir in a large cup of sweet milk, fold in the beaten whites of 2 eggs, put in a deep buttered pan and bake in a slow oven.

Spinach

Cook spinach as usual. Strain and run cold water over it in colander. Press well, then turn out on board, mince it finely and add sufficient flour to make it pretty thick. Then add a teacupful of milk, pepper and salt. Simmer 10 minutes or ¼ hour to cook the flour, then serve.

Vegetable Broth

Put into a pan 2 quarts of water, ½ teacupful of rice or barley; let it boil; add a small quantity of mixed vegetables, such as lettuce, carrot, turnip, parsnip, leeks, celery, parsley and peas; wash and cut the vegetables small; add 1 carrot grated, and simmer for 4 hours, season with pepper and salt.

Watercress

After being picked, watercress should be first put in salted cold water to rid it of all insects, and then thoroughly rinsed in fresh water, and well drained afterwards.

Aspic

Put 1 quart stock, whites and shells of 3 eggs, 1 onion sliced, carrot, 1 tablespoonful vinegar, 1 teaspoonful salt, ½ teaspoonful pepper, 2 oz. leaf gelatine, juice and rind of 1 lemon and 4 cloves into a saucepan, slightly beating the egg with a little of the stock; stir with whisk until it boils. Remove the whisk, and let the froth boil up to the top of the saucepan. Cover, and let it stand ten minutes to clear. Then pour through the jelly-bag, first pouring boiling water to warm the bag. Use for savoury, garnish, etc.

Cress Salad

1 pint water cress   French dressing
1 onion

Pick over the leaves of the cress carefully, removing all bruised or wilted ones, wash and drain, and with the fingers break the stems into two-inch lengths. Lay the cress in a salad bowl, chop the onion very fine, strew it over the cress, add French dressing and serve.

Cress and Dandelion Salad

1 cup water cress   6 thin slices raw onion
1 cup dandelion greens   French dressing

The dandelion should be fresh and young. Wash the leaves carefully and drain well. Arrange them in a salad bowl with the cress. Add the slices of onion and pour the French dressing over all.

For this couple of 1890, the hardest times were over but they may have remembered the time when the only way to cook was in the fireplace; when there was no window glass to be had; when hand-whittled pegs were used for nails. *Courtesy of the Seattle Historical Society*

Engraved for the American Agriculturist.

Kinds of Fruit—A Botanical Description.

BY T. D. BENNETT.

The organs of a flower are of two kinds (1st,) the *protecting* organs or leaves of the flower, consisting of two circles of leaves, the outer called the *calyx*, the inner the *corolla*. (2nd,) The *essential* organs, which are also of two kinds, *stamens* and *pistils* placed one above or within the other. The stamen consists of two parts, the filaments or stem, and the anther, a case which contains the yellow fertilizing dust, called *pollen*. The pistil is in three parts, (beginning from below,) the *ovary*, a hollow case containing rudimentary seeds called the *ovules*, second the *style*, the tapering part above, third the *stigma*, the tip of the style consisting of loose tissue, upon which the pollen falls, when the ripe anthers open. Referring to the flower (1) in the engraving—(a) is the calyx, (b) corolla, (c) stamens, (d) the pistil, with the ovary showing the ovules within. The pollen upon being discharged from the anthers falls upon the stigma and communicates an influence down the style into the ovary: the ovules thus fertilized become seeds, which ripening, with the ovary, constitute the fruit. Proper fruit then is this ripened ovary called seed-vessel or *pericarp*, containing the seeds. Sometimes the calyx (a) adheres to the ovary and thus becomes a part of the fruit, and even forms the principal bulk of it, as in the apple.

Fruits are divided into simple and multiple. Fruits of the former class consist each of a single ovary, one or many seeded, and are classified as Fleshy fruits, Stone fruits, and Dry fruits, etc.

In FLESHY FRUIT the walls of the ovary thicken and become soft and juicy. The principal kinds of fleshy fruits are the following:

The *Berry* which is fleshy or pulpy throughout. The grape, gooseberry (3), currant, tomato, etc., are good examples. The orange, the lemon, the shaddock, etc., are berries with leathery rinds.

The *Pepo*, or *Gourd fruit* (15), is also a sort of berry, externally firm, and internally pulpy. Cucumbers, melons, and squashes are illustrations.

In the *Pome* (2), such as the apple, pear, and quince, the calyx only is thickened, the star-like core in the center is the ripened ovary.

Of STONE FRUITS the most familiar kind is the *Drupe* (11), such as the cherry, plum and peach. In this, the outer part of the ovary becomes fleshy, like a berry, while the inner hardens like a nut. The blackberry and raspberry are composed of a great number of miniature stone fruits, like cherries, upon an elongated *receptacle*, as the end of the flower stalk is called.

In DRY FRUIT, the seed-vessel remains herbaceous in texture, or becomes thin; or else it hardens throughout. Some forms are *indehiscent*, that is, remain closed; others are *dehiscent*, that is, split open at maturity in some regular way. The principal indehiscent kinds are the following:

The *Achenium*, or Akene. This may be mistaken for a naked seed; but it is a ripened ovary, the remains of its stigma being plainly seen. Of this sort is the fruit of the Buttercup (13). The crown on the top of some species of akene fruit is called *Pappus*; in some it represents a cup, in others, scales, as in the sunflower (9); in the thistle, aster, dandelion (6), and hundreds of others it is cut up into a tuft of fine hairs.

The *Utricle* is the same as an akene, with a thin, bladdery pericarp; as seen in the pigweed (12).

A *Caryopsis* or Grain differs from the last by the seed filling out and adhering to the pericarp, so that fruit and seed are in one body; as seen in wheat, Indian corn and other kinds of grain.—A *Nut* is a dry indehiscent fruit, commonly one-celled and one-seeded, with a hard bony wall or shell, such as cocoanut, hazlenut and acorn (7).—A *Samara*, or *Key fruit*, is either a nut or an akene, furnished with a wing, like maple keys and seeds of the ash, (17), and elm.—The *Capsule*, or *Pod*, is the general name for dry seed-vessels which split open at maturity. There are several sorts distinguished by particular names. Two have simple pistils, namely:

The *Follicle*, a simple fruit opening as in larkspur, columbine, marsh marigold (5), and the *Legume*, a true pod like the pea (4), this is similar to the follicle only it opens at both sides.

The true *Capsule* is the pod of a compound pistil. The difference between a simple and compound pistil can be seen by comparing the pea (4), and marsh marigold (5), with the triangular fruit of the Iris, or Flower de Luce, (18).

The *Silique* (16), the pod of the mustard family, differs from the legume by having a so-called false partition, to which the seeds are attached.

The *Pyxis* is a pod which opens by a horizontal line, one part forming a lid, as in purslane (10).

Multiple or *Collective Fruits* are masses of fruit, resulting from several blossoms, aggregated into one body, as the pineapple, mulberry, and fig.

The *Strobile* or *Cone* is a scaly multiple fruit. The hop is one species where the large scales are bracts; but the name more especially belongs to the pine or fir cone. The scales are *open pistils* overlying each other and pressed together in a spike; 14 is one of these scales of a pine cone.

In this description all the principal kinds of fruit are embraced. Those who may wish a more elaborate description we will refer to Gray's Botanical Text Book. The sketch accompanying is furnished to the *Agriculturist* from a Botanical Plate, probably to be published.

Dahlia Hoops.

A very simple and apparently practical contrivance has been left upon the exhibition tables of the *American Agriculturist*, by Mr. Andrew W. Nicholson, of Brooklyn. A stout wire is bent in the form shown, so that placing the curved parts of the wire against a plant stake, and passing a barrel hoop through the other looped ends of the wire behind the stake, it may be securely fastened at any elevation on the stake by a wedge placed between the hoop and the stake as represented. The ends of the hoops are secured by two rings of tin or zinc, which allow them to slide freely through, and the hoop thus be enlarged or contracted at pleasure.

JELLIES AND PRESERVES

Pectin, a carbohydrate somewhat similar in its properties to starch, is found in all fruits when ripe or nearly so. It is because of this substance in the fruit juice that we are able to make jelly. When equal quantities of sugar and fruit juice are combined and the mixture is heated to the boiling point for a short time, the pectin in the fruit gelatinizes in the mass.

An acid fruit is the most suitable for jelly making, though in some of the acid fruits, the strawberry for example, the quantity of the jelly-making pectin is so small that it is difficult to make jelly of this fruit. If, however, some currant juice be added to the strawberry juice, a pleasant jelly will be the result, yet, of course, the flavour of the strawberry will be modified. Here is a list of the most desirable fruits for jelly making. The very best are given first: Currant, crab apple, apple, quince, grape, blackberry, raspberry, peach. For the inexperienced jelly maker the safe rule is to confine jelly-making to the fruits which are ideal for the purpose.

In making jelly with the juice of currants and under-ripe grapes use 1 cup of sugar to 1 cup of juice. With raspberries, blackberries, blueberries, sour apples, crab apples, quinces, wild cherries and green gooseberries use ¾ cup of sugar to 1 cup of juice. This applies to the first extraction of juice and to the later extractions when they have been boiled to the consistency of the first extraction.

Satisfactory jelly may be made by using ½ to ⅓ cup corn syrup or honey to 1 cup of fruit juice, following the general directions for jelly making. The proportion of sugar substitute will depend upon the acidity and pectin content of the fruit juice. On account of the water content of the corn syrup the juice will require a little longer cooking before the jelly point is reached. Fruits which contain pectin but lack sufficient acid are peach, pear, quince, sweet apple and guava. With these acid may be added by the use of juice of sour apples, crab apples or under-ripe grapes.

Strawberries and cherries have acidity but lack pectin. The pectin may be supplied by the addition of the juices mentioned above.

Apples make a very mild jelly, and it may be flavoured with fruits, flowers, or spices. If the apples are acid it is not advisable to use any flavor.

Juicy fruits, such as currants, raspberries, etc., should not be gathered after a rain, for they will have absorbed so much water as to make it difficult, without excessive boiling, to get the juice to jell.

If berries are sandy or dusty it will be necessary to wash them but the work should be done very quickly so that the fruit may not absorb much water.

Large fruits, such as apples, peaches, and pears, must be boiled in water until soft. The strained liquid will contain the flavoring matter and pectin.

In the case of the large fruits a fair estimate is 3 quarts of strained juice from 8 quarts of fruit and about 4 quarts of water. If the quantity of juice is greater than this it should be boiled down to 3 quarts.

Apples will always require 4 quarts of water to 8 quarts of fruit, but juicy peaches and plums will require only 3 or 3½ quarts.

The jelly will be clearer and finer if the fruit is simmered gently and not stirred during the cooking.

It is always best to strain the juice first through cheese cloth and without pressure. If the cloth is doubled the juice will be quite clear. When a very clear jelly is desired the strained juice should pass through a flannel or felt bag. To make a flannel bag, take a square piece of flannel (27 by 27 inches is a good size) fold it to make a three-cornered bag, stitch one of the sides, cut the top square across, bind the opening with strong, broad tape, stitch on this binding four tapes with which to tie the bag to a frame. To use this bag, tie it to a frame or to the backs of two kitchen chairs. If the chairs are used, place some heavy articles in them; or the bag may hang on a pole (a broom handle) which rests on the backs of the chairs. A high stool turned upside down makes a good support for the bag. Put a bowl on the floor under the bag, then pour in the fruit juice, which will pass through comparatively clear. Before it is used the bag should be washed and boiled in clear water.

A cause of the jelly crystallizing is hard boiling. When the sirup boils so rapidly that particles of it are thrown on the upper part of the sides of the preserving kettle they often form crystals. If these crystals are stirred into the sirup they are apt to cause the mass to crystallize in time. The use of the sirup gauge and care not to boil the sirup too violently would do away with all uncertainty in jelly making. The sirup gauge should register 25° no matter what kind of fruit is used.

After jelly is prepared, sterilize glasses; take from the boiling water and set them on a shallow baking pan in which there is about 2 inches of boiling water.

Covering Jellies

Jellies are so rich in sugar that they are not subject to spoilage by bacteria and yeasts, but they must be covered carefully to protect them from mold spores and evaporation. To cover, have disks of thick white paper the size of the top of the glass. When the jelly is set, brush the top over with brandy or alcohol. Dip a disk of paper in the spirits and put it on the jelly. If the glasses have covers, put them on. If there are no covers, cut disks of paper about half an inch in diameter larger than the top of the glass. Beat together the white of one egg and a tablespoonful of cold water. Wet the paper covers with this mixture and put over the glass, pressing down the sides well to make them stick to the glass; or the covers may be dipped in olive oil and be tied on the glasses, but they must be cut a little larger than when the white of egg is used. A thick coating of paraffin makes a good cover, but not quite so safe as the paper dipped in brandy or alcohol, because the spirits destroy any mold spores that may happen to rest on the jelly. If such spores are covered with the paraffin they may develop under it. If paraffin is used, break it into pieces and put in a cup. Set the cup in a pan of warm water on the back of the stove. In a few moments it will be melted enough to cover the jelly. Have the coating about a fourth of an inch thick. In cooling the paraffin contracts, and if the layer is very thin it will crack and leave a portion of the jelly exposed.

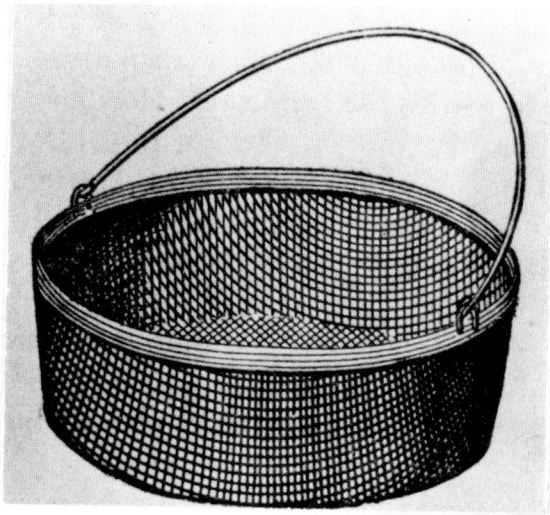

Wire Basket

Fruits to be peeled can be placed into a wire basket and lowered into a deep kettle partially filled with boiling water. After a few minutes the basket is lifted from the boiling water, plunged into cold water, then the fruit is ready to have the skin drawn off.

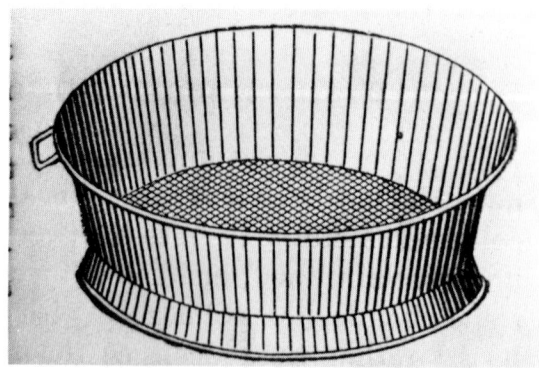

Wire Sieve

A strong wire sieve is a necessity when purées of fruit are to be made. These sieves are known as purée sieves. They are made of strong wire and in addition have supports of still stronger wire.

Apple Jelly

Wash, stem, and wipe the apples, being careful to clean the blossom end thoroughly. Cut into quarters and put into the preserving kettle. Barely cover with cold water (about 4 quarts of water to 8 of apples) and cook gently until the apples are soft and clear. Strain the juice and proceed as for currant jelly. There should be but 3 quarts of juice from 8 quarts of apples and 4 of water. Apples vary in the percentage of sugar and acid they contain. A fine-flavored acid apple should be employed when possible. Apple jelly may be made at any time of the year, but winter apples are best and should be used when in their prime, i.e., from the fall to December or January. When it is found necessary to make apple jelly in the spring, add the juice of one lemon to every pint of apple juice.

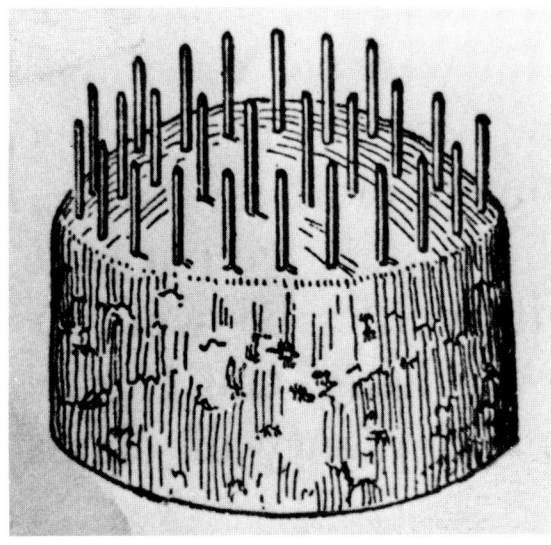

Fruit Pricker

A fruit pricker is easily made and saves time. Cut a piece half an inch deep from a broad cork; press through this a dozen or more coarse darning needles; tack the cork on a piece of board. Strike the fruit on the bed of needles, and you have a dozen holes at once. When the work is finished, remove the cork from the board, wash and dry thoroughly. A little oil on the needles will prevent rusting. With needles of the size suggested there is little danger of the points breaking, but it is worth remembering the use of pricking machines was abandoned in curing prunes on a commercial scale in California because the steel needles broke and remained in the fruit.

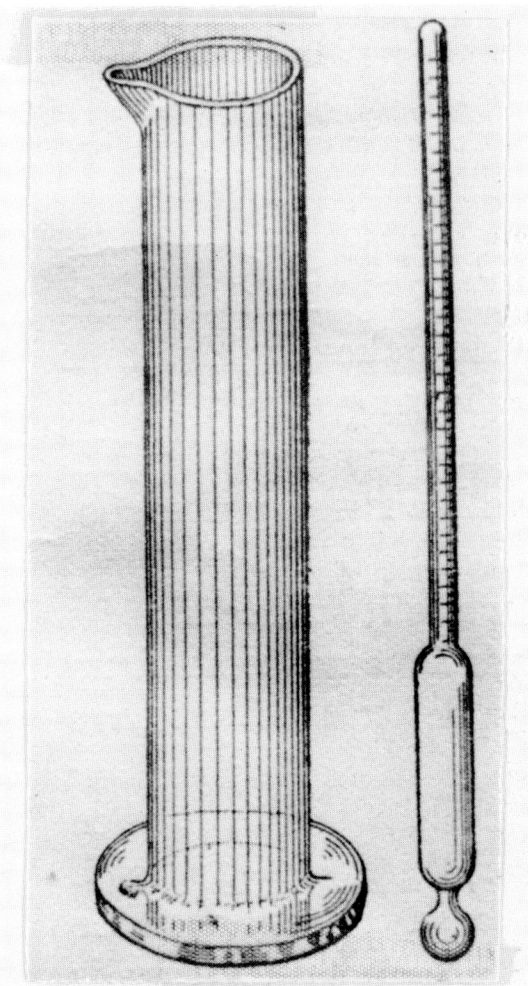

Syrup Gauge

A sirup gauge and glass cylinder are not essential to preserving, canning, and jelly making, but they are valuable aids in getting the right proportion of sugar for fruit or jelly. The sirup gauge costs about 50 cents and the cylinder about 25 cents. A lipped cylinder that holds a little over a gill is the best size. If this gauge is placed in pure water the bulb will rest on the bottom of the cylinder or other container. If sugar be dissolved in the water the gauge will begin to float. The more sugar there is dissolved in the water the higher the gauge will rise. In making tests it is essential that the sirup should be deep enough to reach the zero point of the gauge. If a glass cylinder holding about half a gill is filled to about two-thirds its height, and the gauge is then placed in the cylinder, the quantity of sugar in the sirup will be registered on the gauge.

Blackberry Jelly

Make the same as currant jelly.

Black-Currant or Gooseberry Jam

Weight for weight of sugar and fruit, and to every 6 pounds of fruit add ½ pint red-currant juice. Boil from 10 to 15 minutes.

Crab-Apple Jelly

Make the same as plain apple jelly.

Cider Apple Jelly

Make the same as plain apple jelly, but covering the apples with cider instead of water. The cider must be fresh from the press.

Currant Jelly

The simplest method of making currant jelly is perhaps the following: Free the currants from leaves and large stems. Put them in the preserving kettle; crush a few with a wooden vegetable masher or spoon; heat slowly, stirring frequently. When the currants are hot, crush them with the vegetable masher. Put a hair sieve or strainer over a large bowl; over this spread a double square of cheese cloth. Turn the crushed fruit and juice into the cheese cloth, and let it drain as long as it drips, but do not use pressure. To hasten the process take the corners of the straining cloth firmly in the hands and lift from the sieve; move the contents by raising one side of the cloth and then the other. After this put the cloth over another bowl. Twist the ends together and press out as much juice as possible. This juice may be used to make a second quality of jelly.

To make currant jelly by the cold process follow the first rule for jelly as far as dissolving the sugar in the strained juice. Fill warm, sterilized glasses with this. Place the glasses on a board and put the board by a sunny window. Cover with sheets of glass and keep by the window until the jelly is set. The jelly will be more transparent if the juice is strained through the flannel bag. Jelly made by the cold process is more delicate than that made by boiling, but it does not keep quite so well.

Green Gooseberry Jelly

To 4 pints gooseberries give 3 pints water (always 1 pint less water than gooseberries); boil to a mash, then strain through cheese-cloth. Take 1 pound sugar to every pint of juice, but keep out a little sugar to throw in about 7 minutes before taking it off; this improves the colour wonderfully. Boil ½ hour, then flavour with essence of lemon.

Green-Grape Jelly

Make the same as apple jelly.

Ripe-Grape Jelly

An acid grape is best for this jelly. The sweet, ripe grapes contain too much sugar. Half-ripe fruit, or equal portions of nearly ripe and green grapes will also be found satisfactory. Wild grapes make delicious jelly. Make the same as currant jelly.

Oregon Grape or Salal Jelly

Sort and wash Oregon Grapes or Salal berry. Remove stems or caps. Crush berries and extract 2 cups juice. Sort and wash apples. Remove stems and blossom ends. Do not pare or core but cut into small pieces. Add water, cover and bring to boil on high heat. Reduce heat and simmer until apples are soft. Extract 2 cups juice. Pour juices into kettle. Add 2 tablespoons lemon juice and 3 cups sugar. Stir well. Boil over high heat until jelly mixture sheets from spoon. Remove from heat, skim foam off quickly and pour immediately into hot sterilized containers and seal. Makes 4 to 5 six-ounce glasses.

Parsley Jelly

Take a quantity of fresh parsley, well washed. Put in jelly-pan, cover with cold water, and press down lightly. Boil gently for about ½ hour, and pour it twice through a jelly-bag. To each pint of juice add 1 pound sugar. Boil for about 20 minutes pretty smartly.

Plum Jelly

Use an underripe acid plum. Wash the fruit and remove the stems. Put into the preserving kettle with 1 quart of water for each peck of fruit. Cook gently until the plums are boiled to pieces. Strain the juice and proceed the same as for currant jelly.

Quince Jelly

Rub the quinces with a coarse crash towel; cut out the blossom end. Wash the fruit and pare it and cut in quarters. Cut out the cores, putting them in a dish by themselves. Have a large bowl half full of water; drop the perfect pieces of fruit into this bowl. Put the parings and imperfect parts, cut very fine, into the preserving kettle. Add a quart of water to every 2 quarts of fruit and parings. Put on the fire and cook gently for two hours. Strain and finish the same as apple jelly. The perfect fruit may be preserved or canned. To make quince jelly of a second quality, when the parings and fruit are put on to cook put the cores into another kettle and cover them generously with water and cook two hours. After all the juice has been drained from the parings and fruit, put what remains into the preserving kettle with the cores. Mix well and turn into the straining cloth. Press all the juice possible from this mixture. Put the juice in the preserving kettle with a pint of sugar to a pint of juice; boil ten minutes.

Raspberry and Currant Jelly

Make the same as currant jelly, using half currants and half raspberries.

Raspberry Jelly

Make the same as currant jelly.

Red-Currant Jelly
(Made without boiling.)

Pound and sift 1 pound sugar very finely, and make it very hot in the oven. Strain 1 pint juice from the currants and make the juice also as hot as possible without actually boiling. When the juice is all but boiling (be very careful not to let it boil) take it off the fire and stir the hot sugar in gradually, and keep on stirring till the last moment. When the sugar has entirely melted, the juice is ready to be put into pots. It will jell as well as if boiled and keep the flavour of fresh fruit.

Rose Hip Jelly

Gather rose hips after the first frost. Wash two cups thoroughly and remove ends. Boil for about five minutes in one cup of water. Strain juice in jelly bag overnight. Measure juice and add apple juice; one cup of rose hip juice to three cups of apple juice. Boil together for ten minutes. Add two cups of sugar and continue boiling until it begins to jell. Pour into clean, hot glasses and seal as for any jelly.

Strawberry Jelly

To 10 quarts of strawberries add 2 quarts of currants and proceed as for currant jelly, but boil fifteen minutes.

Fruit Preserves

In the case of most fruits, canning with a little sugar is to be preferred to preserving with a large quantity of sugar. There are, however, some fruits that are only good when preserved with a good deal of sugar. Of course, such preparations of fruit are only desirable for occasional use. The fruits best adapted for preserving are strawberries, sour cherries, sour plums, and quinces. Such rich preparations should be put up in small jars or tumblers.

Cherries

The sour cherries, such as Early Richmond and Montmorency, are best for this preserve. Remove the stems and stones from the cherries and proceed as for strawberry preserve.

Cherries Preserved With Currant Juice

Put 3 quarts of currants in the preserving kettle and on the fire. When they boil up crush them and strain through cheese cloth, pressing out all the juice. Stem and stone 12 quarts cherries, being careful to save all the juice. Put the cherries, fruit juice, and 2 quarts of sugar in the preserving kettle. Heat to the boiling point and skim carefully. Boil for twenty minutes. Put in sterilized jars or tumblers. This gives an acid preserve. The sugar may be doubled if richer preserves are desired.

Plum Preserve

Prick 4 quarts of green gages and put it in a preserving kettle. Cover generously with cold water. Heat to the boiling point and boil gently for five minutes. Drain well.

Put 2 quarts of sugar and 1 pint water in a preserving kettle and stir over the fire until the sugar is dissolved. Boil five minutes, skimming well. Put the drained green gages in this sirup and cook gently for twenty minutes. Put in sterilized jars.

Other plums may be preserved in the same manner. The skins should be removed from white plums.

Quinces

Boil 4 quarts of pared, quartered, and cored quinces in clear water until it is tender, then skim out and drain.

Put the 2 quarts of sugar and 1 quart of water in the preserving kettle; stir until the sugar is dissolved. Let it heat slowly to the boiling point. Skim well and boil for twenty minutes. Pour one-half of the syrup into a second kettle. Put one-half of the cooked and drained fruit into each kettle. Simmer gently for half an hour, then put in sterilized jars. The water in which the fruit was boiled can be used with parings, cores, and gnarly fruit to make jelly.

Quince Preserves

Wash and wipe the quinces. Pare, core and cut into slices, or they may be quartered. Be sure to throw each piece into cold water to prevent discoloration. Put them into the kettle and barely cover with boiling water. Simmer until tender; skim out the fruit very carefully and add the parings but not the cores to the liquid; cover and simmer one hour. Strain and to every pint of this juice allow one pint of sugar; stir until dissolved. Bring quickly to the boiling point and boil hard (if there is a quart of juice) fifteen minutes, skimming well. Now put in the quinces and boil until clear and red. It is better to keep them covered if you wish them bright in color. When the quinces are done skim out into hot sterilized jelly glasses. Boil the juice if necessary a little longer to become thick; pour this over the fruit and stand in the sunshine to finish. Seal as directed.

Strawberry Preserves

Use equal weights of sugar and strawberries. Put the strawberries in the preserving kettle in layers, sprinkling sugar over each layer. The fruit and sugar should not be more than 4 inches deep. Place the kettle on the stove and heat the fruit and sugar slowly to the boiling point. When it begins to boil skim carefully. Boil ten minutes, counting from the time the fruit begins to bubble. Pour the cooked fruit into platters, having it about 2 or 3 inches deep. Place the platters in a sunny window, in an unused room, for three or four days. In that time the fruit will grow plump and firm, and the sirup will thicken almost to a jelly. Put this preserve, cold, into jars or tumblers.

Rose Hip Preserves

Gather and clean. Simmer two cups of rose hips in four cups of water until soft. Wash crab apples and cook to a pulp. Combine and put through a colander to remove seeds. Measure pulp and add one cup sugar for each cup of pulp. Cook until as thick as desired.

Tomato Preserves

Scald and peel carefully some small tomatoes (yellow preferred) add an equal weight of sugar and let stand over night; pour off all the juice and boil until it is a thick syrup; add tomatoes and boil until transparent. A piece of ginger root or 1 lemon, sliced thin, to a pound of fruit is a good addition.

White Currants

Select large, firm fruit, remove the stems, and proceed as for strawberries.

Fruit Butters

Fruit butters may be made from good sound fruits or the sound portions of fruits which are wormy or have been bruised. Wash, pare and remove seeds if there are any. Cover with water and cook 3 to 4 hours at a low temperature, stirring often, until the mixture is of the consistency of thick apple sauce. Add sugar, syrup or honey to taste when the boiling is two-thirds done. Spices may be added to suit the taste when the boiling is completed. If the pulp is coarse it should be put through a wire sieve or colander. Pour the butter into sterilized jar, put on rubber and cover and adjust top bail. Put into a container having a cover and false bottom. Pour in an inch or so of water and sterilize quart jar or smaller jar 5 minutes after the steam begins to escape. Remove, push snap in place and cool.

Dried Peach Butter

Soak dried peaches over night. Cook slowly until tender. To each 2 pounds of dried peaches add 1 quart of canned peaches and 1¾ pounds of sugar, syrup or honey. If a fine texture is desired, strain pulp through a colander. Cook slowly, stirring often, until thick. Pack in hot jars and sterilize 5 minutes in steam.

Apple Butter With Cider

Four quarts of sweet or sterilized cider should be boiled down to 2 quarts. To this add 4 quarts of apples peeled and cut in small pieces. If the texture of the apples is coarse they should be boiled and put through a strainer before being added to the cider. Boil this mixture until the cider does not separate from the pulp. When two-thirds done add one pound of sugar, syrup or honey. One-half teaspoonful each of cinnamon, allspice and cloves may be added. Pour into sterilized jars and sterilize 5 minutes in steam.

Apple and butter may be made by following the directions for apple butter with cider but omitting the cider.

Apple Butter with Grape Juice

To every 4 quarts of strained apple sauce add 1 pint of grape juice, 1 cup of brown sugar, syrup or honey and ¼ teaspoonful of salt. Cook slowly, stirring often, until of the desired thickness. When done stir in 1 teaspoonful of cinnamon, pack in hot jars and sterilize 5 minutes in steam.

Peach Butter

Dip peaches in boiling water long enough to loosen the skins. Dip in cold water, peel and stone them. If peaches do not peel readily when dipped in boiling water, omit dipping and pare them. Mash and cook them without adding any water. Add half as much sugar, syrup or honey as pulp and cook until thick. Pour into sterilized jars and sterilize 5 minutes in steam.

Plum butter may be made following the directions for peach butter.

Texas Plum Butter

A vat of cane juice is boiled down until it begins to thicken. To the syrup mixture add plums, boil constantly for hours, stirring with a wooden paddle to keep from scorching. Cook until the thickness required. One vat will generally make one-half barrel of butter.

Currant Conserves

One and one-half pounds of stewed currants, six oranges and rinds, juice of one lemon, one pound of chopped raisins, two and one-half pound of sugar.

Gooseberry Conserves

Remove the stems from 6 quarts green gooseberries, and chop 2 pounds seedless raisins rather coarsely. Cut 5 oranges into halves and take out the juice and pulp, removing the seeds; cook peel of 3 of them soft in enough boiling water to cover, changing water once or twice; drain; remove the white part from the peel by scraping with a spoon. Then cut into narrow strips; put 5 pounds sugar, berries, orange peel, juice and rind together in a kettle and heat slowly until the syrup is thick.

Marmalades

Marmalades require great care while cooking because no moisture is added to the fruit and sugar. If the marmalade is made from berries the fruit should be rubbed through a sieve to remove the seeds. If large fruit is used have it washed, pared, cored, and quartered.

Measure the fruit and sugar, allowing one pint of sugar to each quart of fruit. Rinse the preserving kettle with cold water that there may be a slight coat of moisture on the sides and bottom. Put alternate layers of fruit and sugar in the kettle, having the first layer fruit. Heat slowly, stirring frequently. While stirring, break up the fruit as much as possible. Cook about two hours, then put in small sterilized jars.

San Diego Orange Marmalade

Cut off the ends of 6 oranges (navel) and 3 lemons and throw away. Peel thin oranges and lemons round and round like an apple and then cut with shears very fine. Remove the white skin and cut the pulp into fine pieces. Cover the pulp and shredded peel well with cold water and let stand 12 to 24 hours. Drain, add the water and cook until reduced one inch or until the rinds are tender. Add equal amount of sugar and cook until it jellies.

Compote of Mixed Fruits

Strawberries, grapes, raspberries, green figs, melon, pineapple, etc. Cut up the larger fruits, and sift a little sugar over all in a dish. Make a syrup by boiling 1 pound sugar and 1½ pints water till reduced to a pint. Pour over fruit while hot and stand in cool place for 24 hours. Turn out into glass bowl and serve very cold. Make plenty of syrup so that fruit floats about in it.

At the first opportunity, fruit trees were planted and the juicy reward hopefully anticipated. Oftentimes the trees were watered by hand. This is a picture of a young orchard taken in 1911. *Courtesy of the Washington State University, Henderson Collection*

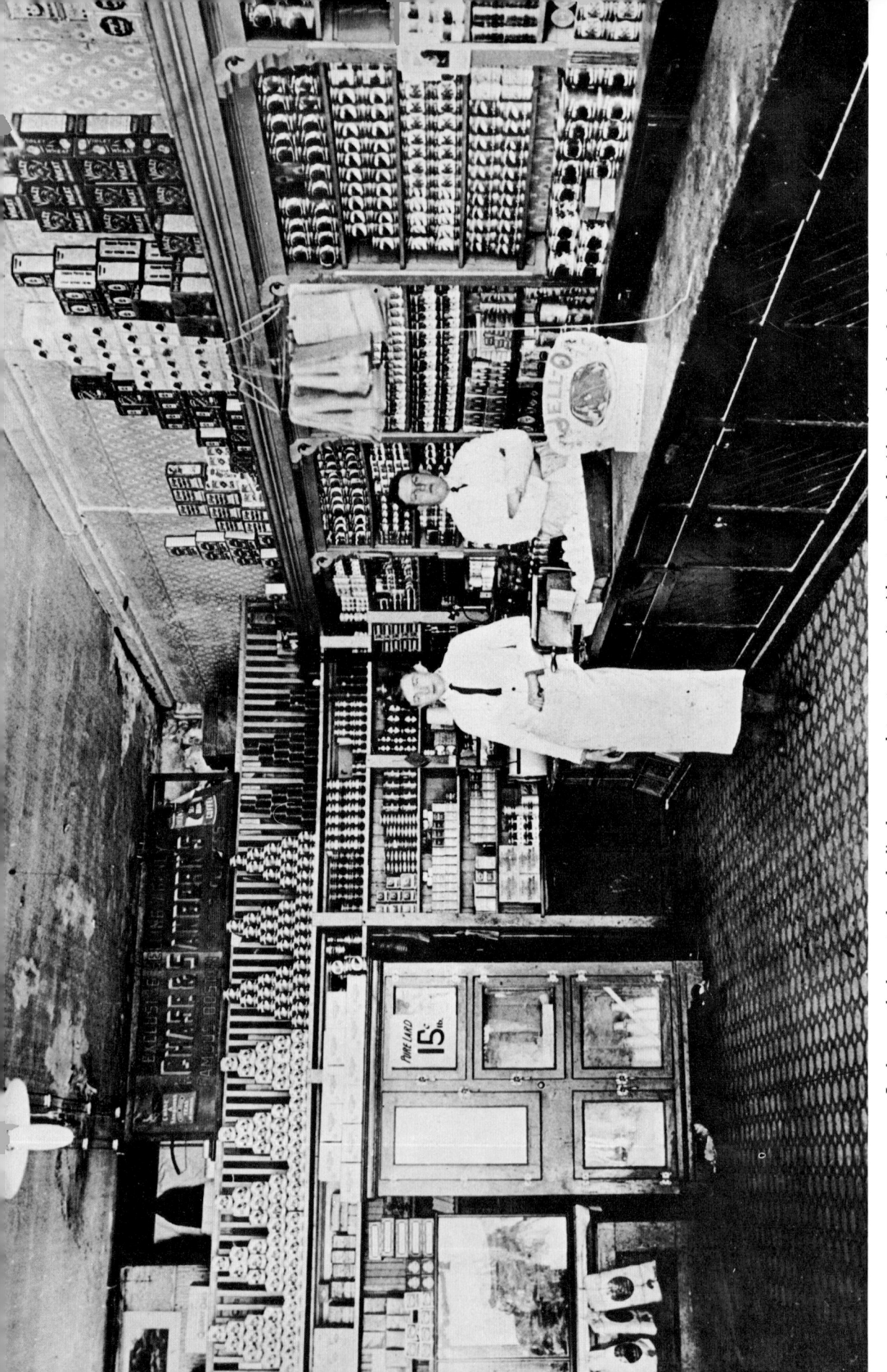

Lucky were the homesteaders who lived near enough to a town or city with a store stocked with canned and packaged goods. This store interior was photographed in 1912-1914 period. *Courtesy of the Seattle Historical Society*

Fruit Preserved in Grape Juice

Any kind of fruit can be preserved by this method, but it is particularly good for apples, pears, and sweet plums. No sugar need be used in this process. Boil 6 quarts of grape juice in an open preserving kettle, until it is reduced to 4 quarts. Have the fruit washed and pared, and, if apples or pears, quartered and cored. Put the prepared fruit in a preserving kettle and cover generously with the boiled grape juice. Boil gently until the fruit is clear and tender, then put in sterilized jars.

Fruit Purées

Purées of fruit are in the nature of marmalades, but they are not cooked so long, and so retain more of the natural flavor of the fruit. This is a particularly nice way to preserve the small, seedy fruits, which are to be used in puddings, cake, and frozen desserts.

Free the fruit from leaves, stems, and decayed portions. Peaches and plums should have the skins and stones removed. Rub the fruit through a purée sieve. To each quart of the strained fruit add a pint of sugar. Pack in sterilized jars. Put the covers loosely on the jars. Place the jars in the rack in the boiler. Pour in enough cold water to come half way up the sides of the jars. Heat gradually to the boiling point and boil thirty minutes, counting from the time when the water begins to bubble.

Have some boiling sirup ready. As each jar is taken from the boiler put it in a pan of hot water and fill up with the hot sirup. Seal at once.

Boiled Cider

When the apple crop is abundant and a large quantity of cider is made, the housekeeper will find it to her advantage to put up a generous supply of boiled cider. Such cider greatly improves mincemeat, and can be used at any time of the year to make cider apple sauce. It is also a good selling article.

The cider for boiling must be perfectly fresh and sweet. Put it in a large, open preserving kettle and boil until it is reduced one-half. Skim frequently while boiling. Do not have the kettle more than two-thirds full. Put in bottles or stone jugs.

Cider Apple Sauce

Put 8 quarts of pared, quartered, and cored sweet apples in a large preserving kettle and cover with 5 quarts boiled cider. Cook slowly until the apples are clear and tender. To prevent burning, place the kettle on an iron tripod or ring. It will require from two to three hours to cook the apples. If you find it necessary to stir the sauce be careful to break the apples as little as possible. When the sauce is cooked, put in sterilized jars.

In the late spring, when cooking apples have lost much of their flavor and acidity, an appetizing sauce may be made by stewing them with diluted boiled cider, using 1 cupful of cider to 3 of water.

Clear Apples

Make a syrup by boiling 8 oz. lump sugar and 1 pint water together for ¼ hour. Pare and core 8 large apples, keeping them whole; put them as you pare them in cold water to keep them white. Put apples in pan, pour the boiling syrup over, and leave on the fire for a few minutes. Take out carefully and place on glass dish. Make a syrup pink, with a few drops cochineal, and pour it over the apples. Serve cold, with a teaspoonful whipped cream on each apple.

Cider Pear Sauce

Cooking pears may be preserved in boiled cider the same as sweet apples. If one prefers the sauce less sour, 1 pint of sugar may be added to each quart of boiled cider.

Spiced Currants

Wash and stem currants, then measure out 1 quart. Put 1 pint vinegar into the kettle and 3 pounds sugar, stirring until well dissolved. Add the fruit and 1 tablespoonful each ground cloves, ground cinnamon, ground allspice and boil two hours. This may boil more slowly than for jams, but must be watched and stirred often so that it does not burn nor stick.

Ripe cherries and gooseberries are delicious spiced in this manner and all are nice to serve with cold meats.

Pioneer Merchants such as this, sold among their articles, fancy goods, albums, toilet cases, toys, purses, rocking horses, doll buggies, children's wagons, tobacco, cigars, playing cards, pocket knives, chips, fishing tackle, baby buggies, and hammocks in addition to staple food items and hardware.

To Keep Cranberries

Put them into a keg of water and they may be kept all winter.

To Keep Grapes

The simplest way is to keep them in drawers or boxes which hold about twenty-five pounds each, and pile them one above another. A better way is to hang a barrel hoop from the ceiling by three cords; seal the stem with sealing wax, attach a wire to the small end of the bunch and hang on the hoop, taking care that no two bunches touch. The imperfect grapes should previously have been picked off. The room should not be too moist and yet not so dry as to wither the grapes and it should be free of frost.

Fruit Sirups

The only difference between sirups and juice is that in the sirup there must be at least half as much sugar as fruit juice.

These sirups are used for flavoring ice creams and water ices. They also make a delicious drink, when two or three spoonfuls are added to a glass of ice water.

Ginger Pears

Two dozen pears, four pounds sugar, one and one-half lemons peeled, one-half pounds crystallized ginger. Boil like preserves.

Mrs. C. S. Cotton and Maude Moale, Ca. 1900. In the 'horse and buggy days' it was the custom to go to bed with the sun unless there was a social function or dance to attend. Guests went on horseback, sometimes two on one horse, buggy or wagon, arrived at sundown and stayed until daybreak the next day. Those were 'great times.' *Courtesy of the Seattle Historical Society*

SUN DRYING, FERMENTATION, PICKLING, VINEGAR

Sun Drying Vegetables and Fruits

Sun drying has the double advantage of requiring no expense for fuel and of freedom from danger of overheating. The sun drying of vegetables and fruits the simplest form is to spread the slices or pieces on sheets of plain paper or lengths of muslin nailed to strips of wood and expose them to the sun. Muslin is to be preferred if there is danger of sticking. Trays should be used for larger quantities. Sun drying requires bright, hot days and a breeze. Once or twice a day the product should be turned or stirred and the dry pieces taken out. The drying product should be covered with cheesecloth tacked to a frame for protection from dust and flying insects. Care must be taken to provide protection from rain, dew and moths. During rains and just before sunset the products should be taken indoors for protection.

Preparing Material For Drying

A sharp knife will serve every purpose in slicing and cutting vegetables and fruits for drying if no other device is at hand. The thickness of the slices should be from an eighth to a quarter of an inch. Whether sliced or cut into strips the pieces should be small so as to dry quickly. They should not, however, be so small as to make them hard to handle or to keep them from being used to advantage in preparing dishes for the table such as could be prepared from fresh products. Food choppers, crout slicers or rotary slicers may be used to prepare food for drying.

Vegetables and fruits for drying should be fresh, mature and in prime condition for eating. As a general rule vegetables will dry better if cut into small pieces with the skins removed. Berries are dried whole. Apples, quinces, peaches and pears dry better if cut into rings or quarters. Cleanliness is imperative. Knives and slicing devices must be carefully cleansed before and after use. A knife that is not bright and clean will discolor the product on which it is used and this should be avoided.

Blanching

Blanching is desirable for successful vegetable drying. It is done by placing the vegetables in a piece of cheesecloth, a wire basket or other porous container and plunging them into boiling water. A more desirable way is to blanch in steam. For small quantities a pail or deep kettle is serviceable. A false bottom raised an inch or more is necessary. Upon this rests a wire basket or cheesecloth filled with the prepared vegetables. The water should be just below the false bottom and be boiling vigorously when the products are put in. Cover with a tight-fitting cover. Keep the water boiling during the blanching period. For larger quantities a wash-boiler partially filled with water is convenient. Bricks set on end or a wooden frame raised a few inches above the water make good supports for the containers.

In addition to exercising great care to protect vegetables and fruits from insects during the drying process, precautions should be taken with the finished product to prevent the hatching of eggs that may have been deposited. One measure that is useful is to subject the dried material to a heat of 180° F. for from 5 to 10 minutes.

Put the dried products in bins, boxes, or, if the quantity is small, in bowls. Once a day for a period of ten days to two weeks, stir thoroughly or pour from one box to another. The containers should be in a clean, dry room, and protected from light and insects. Shutters and screens at the window are desirable. Otherwise protect the dried food by spreading clean cloths over it. If any part of the material is found to be moist, after this process, return it to the drier for a short time. When for several days no change in the moisture content has been noticed, and therefore no extra drying has been necessary, the products are ready to be stored.

Of importance equal to proper drying is the proper packing and storage of the finished product. With the scarcity of tins and the high prices of glass jars it is recommended that other containers be used. Those easily available are baking-powder cans and similar covered tins, pasteboard boxes having tight-fitting covers, strong paper bags, and patented paraffin paper boxes, which may be bought in quantities at comparatively low cost.

A paraffin container of the type used by oyster dealers for the delivery of oysters will be found inexpensive and easily handled. If using this, or a baking-powder can or similar container, after filling adjust the cover closely. For storage on a larger scale use closely built wooden boxes with well-fitted lids. Line each box with paraffin paper in several layers. The paper should cover the top of the contents.

It is essential that the container should exclude light and insects but it should not be air-tight. Products stored in air-tight containers suffer damage through moisture which escapes from the product and condenses in the package. If a paper bag is used, the top should be twisted, doubled over and tied with a string. Another good precaution is to store bags within an ordinary lard pail or can or other tin vessel having a fairly close-fitting cover.

The products should be stored in a warm, dry place, well ventilated and protected from rats, mice and insects.

In preparing dried vegetables and fruits for use the first process is to restore the water which has been dried out of them. All dried foods require soaking. After soaking the dried products will have a better flavor if cooked in a covered utensil at a low temperature for a long time.

There can be no definite rule for the amount of water required for soaking dried products when they are to be used, as the quantity of water evaporated in the drying process varies with different vegetables and fruits.

Celery

After washing, carefully cut into even-length pieces—¾ inch or 1 inch is a good measure. Blanch 3 minutes in steam or 2 minutes in boiling water. Drain well, and spread on drying trays in ½ inch layers.

Garden Peas

If the pods are dusty, wash well before shelling. Garden peas with non-edible pod are taken when the size suitable for table use. Blanch 3 to 5 minutes according to size, then drain and spread on drying trays. A depth of ¾ to 1 inch is practicable, but single layers will dry quicker.

Beets, Carrots and Parsnips

Wash well, scrape off skin, and cut into slices of a uniform thickness—3/16 to ¼ inch. Blanch 2 minutes in steam or boiling water. Drain well, spread on drying trays, and dry. These products are sufficiently dry when the pieces break if an effort is made to bend them, and when no moisture shows if they are pressed between the fingers.

Cabbage

Take heads which are well developed. Remove all loose outside leaves and central stalk. Shred or cut into strips a few inches long. Blanch in steam 3 minutes, or in boiling water 4 minutes. Use a wire basket, fill not more than 6 to 8 inches deep; and stir well during the process. When drying, spread in layers not over 1 inch deep, and stir frequently until the product is dry enough not to stick together in close masses.

Lima Beans

Choose mature beans. Shell and blanch 3 minutes in boiling water, keeping the beans well stirred by the motion of the rapidly bubbling water. Drain to remove surface moisture. Spread in thin layers on drying trays, and stir occasionally during the drying process.

Shell Beans and Peas

Beans of different kinds, after maturing and drying on the vines, and being shelled, should be heated to 165° to 180° F. for 10 to 15 minutes to destroy any insect eggs which may be in them. This may be done in an oven. These heated beans cannot be used for planting, because they are devitalized and will not grow. Store in a dry place in bags.

Mature lima beans need only be shelled and stored in bags. Cow peas or any field pea can be treated in the same way.

Sweet Corn

Select ears that are at the milk stage, prime for table use and freshly gathered. Blanch on cob in boiling water for 8 to 12 minutes to set milk. Drain thoroughly, and with a sharp knife cut off in layers or cut off half the kernel and scrape off the remainder, taking care not to include the chaff.

Corn is dry when it is hard and semitransparent.

Fruit Drying

Provide a box large enough to enclose a stack of trays. This may be a packing box or a frame covered with canvas, building paper or wall-board. Stack the filled trays on bricks or blocks of wood which will hold the bottom tray several inches above the ground. The trays should be separated from each other by blocks of wood. Beneath this stack place one or two sticks of sulphur in an old sauce pan, shovel or other holder. Set fire to this sulphur by using coals or lighted shavings and invert the box to cover trays and reach to the ground. Add sulphur as needed during the time specified in the directions.

Apples and Pears

Pare, core and slice, dropping slices into cold water containing eight level teaspoonfuls of salt to the gallon, if a light-colored product is desired. Leaving them for a short time in salt water will prevent discoloration. To sulphur spread in trays of wire 1 to $1\frac{1}{2}$ inches deep. Put each tray in soon as filled into the sulphuring box for 20 to 30 minutes. When the product feels moist on the surface and shows a lightened color, the sulphuring is complete. Begin drying. Stir or rearrange fruit occasionally to insure even drying. The fruit is dry when a handful of slices is pressed and separate when released, leaving no moisture on the hand.

Apricots

Select ripe fruit before it drops from the tree. Remove pits by cutting fruit open with a sharp knife. Apricots are usually dried with the skins on. Arrange the halves on trays with pit cavity uppermost, and dry. If desired, they may be sulphured before drying—the time $1\frac{1}{2}$ to 2 hours.

Figs

Select ripe figs and pick over thoroughly. Wash, drain well and spread in single layers on drying trays. If dried in the sun, turn daily, protect from insects by glass or netting, and bring indoors at night. When nearly dry, immerse figs for 2 or 3 minutes in boiling brine ($\frac{1}{4}$ pound salt to every 3 quarts water, or 1 pound to 3 gallons). Drain, and finish the drying.

Peaches

Select fruit which is uniformly and fully ripe. Cut open with a sharp knife and remove the pits. Peaches are not usually pared, as the juice is lost by dripping if this is done. To sulphur arrange in single layers on trays with the pit surface up. Sulphuring will take from 1-2 hours and is complete when the juice collects in the pit. Care must be taken when transferring trays to drier to prevent loss of juice.

Properly dried peaches are pliable and leathery.

Plums

Select fruit which is ripe. Remove pits by cutting fruit open with a sharp knife. Arrange halves on trays in single layer with pit cavity uppermost. Treat with sulphur fumes 20 to 25 minutes. When liquid collects in the pit cavity the plums are sulphured enough, and are ready to dry.

Properly dried plums are leathery and pliable.

Prunes

Prunes which are fully ripe and have fallen from the trees are best for drying. Grade and dip into boiling lye for 16 to 20 seconds. Allow 1 oz. lye to 2 gallons water. When dipped long enough there will be a slight indication of cracking of the skin near the stem end, but the skin will not be broken. Too strong lye or too long a dip will cause the skin to split and peel off. Rinse thoroughly in cold water and then spread on drying trays in single layers. Properly dried prunes show no moisture when cut or when pressed between the fingers.

Cherries

Stone the cherries carefully through the end, that you may not destroy the appearance of the fruit, and put into a preserving-pan with 8 oz. sugar to every pound of fruit. Simmer gently for $\frac{1}{4}$ hour, then pour out in a bowl with the syrup drawn from the fruit and leave for 24 hours. Then simmer again for 10 minutes, take out the cherries, drain them on a sieve, and dry them in the sun or upon a warm stove. Store them in a tin box in layers, with writing-paper between them. They are useful for puddings or dessert dishes.

Berries

It is not advisable to dry such fruits as red raspberries, currants and strawberries, unless no other conservative methods are convenient.

Properly dried berries rattle somewhat when stirred and show no moisture when pressed.

Fermentation and Salting

The use of brine in preparing vegetables for winter use has much to commend it to the household. The fermentation method is general use in Europe, and is becoming better known in this country as a means of making sour-crout and other food products which do not require the containers used for canning. No cooking is required by this process. Salt brine is the one requirement. The product may be kept in any container that is not made of metal and is water-tight. The vital factor in preserving the material is the lactic acid which develops in fermentation. An important feature is that vegetables thus prepared may be served as they are or they may be freshened by soaking in clear water and cooked as fresh vegetables.

Green Beans

When beans are plentiful take a sharp knife and cut up enough to fill a two gallon jar, cut them slant wise and fine. The pole bean variety is much the best, the large green podded sort, comes next. I have never used wax varieties for this. Put down in a jar a two inch layer of beans and a handful of common salt, pound each layer with a potato masher as you would put down sauerkraut until jar is full. Do not salt as much as for cucumber pickles, put on a plate or cover and weigh down until covered with the brine. This need not be done all at once, but at different times as you pick your beans.

To prepare for the table—Take as many as you wish for dinner, wash them and put on to cook with plenty of water. Let this boil once, then pour off. Return beans to stove with fresh water and stew them until tender. Put in two spoonfuls meat drippings and a little vinegar, set on back of stove and let simmer slowly until nearly boiled dry, then serve.

Sour-crout

The outside leaves of the cabbage should be removed, the core cut crosswise several times and shredded very finely with the rest of the cabbage. Either summer growth or fall cabbage may be used. Immediately pack into a barrel, keg or tub, which is perfectly clean, or into an earthenware crock holding four or five gallons. The smaller containers are recommended for household use. While packing distribute salt as uniformly as possible, using 1 pound of salt to 40 pounds of cabbage. Sprinkle a little salt in the container and put in layer of 3 or 4 inches of shredded cabbage and pack down gently with a wooden utensil like a potato masher. Repeat with salt, cabbage and packing until the container is full or the shredded cabbage is all used. Press the cabbage down as tightly as possible and apply a cloth and then a glazed plate or a board cover which will go inside the holder. If using a wooden cover select wood free from pitch, such as basswood. On top of this cover place stones or other weights (using flint or granite and avoiding the use of limestone or sandstone). These weights serve to force brine above cover.

Allow fermentation to proceed for 10 days or two weeks, if the room is warm. In a cellar or other cool place three to five weeks may be required. Skim off the film which forms when fermentation starts and repeat this daily if necessary to keep this film from becoming scum. When gas bubbles cease to arise, if container is tapped, the fermentation is complete. If there is scum it should be removed. As a final step pour melted paraffin over the brine until it forms a layer from $\frac{1}{4}$ to $\frac{1}{2}$ inch thick to prevent the formation of the scum which occurs if the weather is warm or the storage place is not well cooled. This is not necessary unless the crout is to be kept a long time. The crout may be used as soon as the bubbles cease to rise. If scum forms and remains the crout will spoil. Remove scum, wash cloth cover and weights, pour off old brine and add new.

Pickling Vegetables

Pickling is an important branch of home preparedness for the winter months. Pickles have little food value, but they give a flavor to a meal which is liked by many. They should not be given to children.

In pickling, vegetables are usually soaked overnight in a brine made of 1 cup of salt and 1 quart of water. This brine removes the water of the vegetable and so prevents weakening of the vinegar. In the morning the brine is drained off. Alum should not be used to make the vegetables crisp, as it is harmful to the human body. A firm product is obtained if the vegetables are not cooked too long or at too high a temperature.

Spices, unless confined in a bag, give a dark color to the pickles.

Enameled, agate or porcelain-lined kettles should be used when cooking mixtures containing vinegar.

Pickles put in crocks should be well covered with vinegar to prevent molding. Instructions for some of the most commonly used methods are given herewith.

Picililli

One peck green tomatoes, three medium sized cabbages, five onions and four green peppers, two cups chopped celery or two tablespoons celery seed, two tablespoons cinnamon, two or three tablespoons mustard seed, one-half cup sugar, one teaspoon black pepper, vinegar to cover well. Chop tomatoes separate from cabbage, salt to taste and drain both over night. Peppers and onions may be added in the morning, also celery chopped fine, one-half cup grated horse radish. Set the mixture on the back of the stove, after boiling the vinegar, spices and sugar together, pour over the other (hot). Do this for three or four mornings or let it get hot instead. It will keep in the stone jar in which it is cooked.

Tomato Catsup

Boil 4 quarts ripe tomatoes, (boiled and strained), 4 tablespoonfuls of salt, 2 cups of vinegar, 1 level teaspoonful each of cayenne pepper, cinnamon, cloves, allspice, mustard and black pepper, should be enclosed in cloth bag and removed when catsup is done. Put the corks in tightly and apply hot paraffin to the tops with a brush to make an airtight seal.

Pickled Peaches

Pare peaches by pouring hot water over them, then put three cloves in each peach. For one quart of peaches make a syrup of two cups of sugar and one cup of vinegar with some stick cinnamon in it. After syrup boils put in peaches and boil eight minutes.

Table Relish

Chop: 4 quarts of cabbage, 2 quarts of tomatoes, 1 quart to be green, 6 large onions, 2 hot peppers. Add: 2 ounces white mustard seed, 1 ounce of celery seed, ¼ cup of salt, 6 cups of corn syrup, 2 quarts of vinegar. Pour into sterilized jars or bottles and seal while hot.

Chili Sauce

Simmer for 1 hour, 2 dozen ripe tomatoes (dip in boiling water to peel), 6 peppers (3 to be hot), 3 onions, 2/5 cup of corn syrup, 2 tablespoonfuls of salt, 1 teaspoonful each of cloves, nutmeg and allspice, 1 quart of vinegar. Pour into sterilized jars or bottles and seal while hot.

Chili Sauce

Boil the following ingredients together till tender: 12 ripe tomatoes, 4 green peppers, 2 tablespoons sugar, 8 onions, 2 tablespoons salt, 1 quart vinegar.

Chow Chow

Chop 2 pints cucumbers (1 pint to be small ones), 1 cauliflower soaked in salted water for one hour, 2 green peppers, 1 quart onions, into small pieces. Sprinkle 1 cup of salt over them and let stand all night. Drain well in the morning.

For the sauce make a paste of ¼ pound mustard, 1 tablespoonful of turmeric, 4/5 corn syrup, ½ cup of flour, and a little vinegar. Stir this into the 2 quarts warm vinegar and boil until thick. Then the vegetables and simmer for ½ hour. Stir to prevent burning. Put in cans while hot.

Cold Tomato Relish

To 8 quarts firm, ripe tomatoes (scald, cold-dip and then chop in small pieces) add 2 cups chopped onion, 2 cups chopped celery, 2 cups corn syrup, 1 cup white mustard seed, ½ cup salt, 4 chopped peppers, 1 teaspoonful ground mace, 1 teaspoonful black pepper, 4 teaspoonfuls cinnamon, 3 pints vinegar. Mix all together and pack in sterilized jars.

Corn Relish

Steam 6 ears corn. Cut from the cob and add to 1 small head chopped cabbage, 1 large onion, and 2 hot peppers. Mix 2 tablespoonfuls of flour, 1½ cups corn syrup, 1½ tablespoonfuls of mustard, and 2 tablespoonfuls of salt—add 1 pint of vinegar. Add mixture to the vegetables and simmer 30 minutes. Pour into sterilized jars or bottles and seal while hot.

Cucumber Pickles

Soak in brine made of 1 cup of salt to 2 quarts of water for a day and night. Remove from brine, rinse in cold water and drain. Cover with vinegar, add 1 tablespoonful brown sugar, some stick cinnamon, and cloves to every quart of vinegar used; bring to a boil and pack in jars. For sweet pickles use 1 cup of sugar to 1 quart of vinegar.

Green Tomato Pickle

Take 4 quarts of green tomatoes, 4 small onions and 4 green peppers. Slice the tomatoes and onions thin. Sprinkle over them ½ cup of salt and leave overnight in crock or enameled vessel. The next morning drain off the brine. Into a separate vessel put 1 quart of vinegar, 1 level tablespoonful each of black pepper, mustard seed, celery seed, cloves, allspice and cinnamon and 1 cup of corn syrup. Bring to a boil and then add the prepared tomatoes, onions and peppers. Let simmer for 20 minutes. Fill jars and seal while hot.

Green Tomato Pickle

Wash and slice tomatoes. Soak in a brine of ¼ cup of salt to 1 quart of water overnight. Drain well. Put in a crock and cover with vinegar to which have been added stick cinnamon and 1 cup of corn syrup for every quart of vinegar used. Once a day for a week pour off vinegar, heat to boiling and pour over tomatoes again. Cover top of crock with a cloth and put on cover. This cloth should be frequently washed.

Dill Pickles

To make dill pickles follow the directions for fermenting cucumbers. Using alternate layers of dill leaves, whole mixed spices and cucumbers. The top layer should be of beet or grape leaves an inch thick.

Dill Pickles

Fill a 30 gallon barrell divided into 3 layers, top, middle, and bottom, with cucumbers, 6 pounds green dill, 11 pounds salt, 1 quart vinegar and spices. Fill barrell with water and seal.

Mustard Pickles

Wash, cut in small pieces 2 quarts of green tomatoes, 1 cauliflower, 2 quarts of green peppers, 2 quarts of onions and cover with 1 quart of water and ¼ cup of salt. Let stand 1 hour, bring to the boiling point and drain. Mix ½ pound mustard, 1 cup of flour, 4 cups of corn syrup, and vinegar to make a thin paste. Add this paste to 2 quarts of vinegar and cook until thick, stir constantly to prevent burning. Add vegetables, boil 15 minutes and seal in jars.

Pickled Onions

Peel, wash and put in brine, using 2 cups of salt to 2 quarts water. Let stand 2 days, pour off brine. Cover with fresh brine and let stand 2 days longer. Remove from brine wash and pack in jars, cover with hot vinegar to which whole cloves, cinnamon and allspice have been added.

Spiced Crab-Apples

Wash apples, stick 3 or 4 whole cloves in each one and cover with vinegar to which have been added stick cinnamon and 1-3/5 cups corn syrup for every quart of vinegar used. Cook slowly at a low temperature until apples are heated through. These may be put in jar or stone crocks.

Sweet Pickled Peaches

Wipe peaches and stick 3 or 4 whole cloves in each one. Put in jars or crock and cover with hot vinegar, allowing 3-1/5 cups of corn syrup to each quart of vinegar used. Every morning for a week pour off the vinegar, heat to boiling and pour over peaches again. On the last day seal or cover crock well.

Vinegar

Apple Vinegar

Save the clean peelings and cores from sound, not wormy, apples when cutting them up to dry, for canning, or for sauce or pies, put them in a jar, pour boiling water on, place a plate and weight on top and leave over night. Pour the juice off, put in a stone jar, tie a cloth over the top and let stand, adding more from time to time, and keep in a warm place. This makes good vinegar, forming its own mother in a month. If not covered closely, however, the juice sours.

Black-Currant Vinegar

Fill a large jug nearly full with black currants, then fill up with vinegar, and let this stand 8 or 10 days, each day stirring it well and mashing currants. At the end of that time strain off the vinegar, and to every pint add ¾ pound loaf sugar. Boil it until quite clear, taking off the scum as it rises. Let it go quite cold, then bottle it and cork it securely. Good for colds and coughs.

Raspberry Vinegar

Put 4 quarts of raspberries in a bowl and pour over them 2 quarts of vinegar. Cover and set in a cool place for two days. On the second day strain the vinegar through cheese cloth. Put 4 quarts of fresh raspberries in the bowl and pour over them the vinegar strained from the first raspberries. Put in a cool place for two days, then strain. Put the strained juice in a preserving kettle with 3 quarts of sugar. Heat slowly, and when the vinegar boils skim carefully. Boil twenty minutes, then put in sterilized bottles.

About 2 tablespoonfuls of vinegar to a glass of water makes a refreshing drink. Similar vinegars may be made from blackberries and strawberries.

HERBS, PLANTS, ROOTS AND REMEDIES

How to Gather and Keep

Gather on a dry day, and just before they flower. Cut off roots and free from dust, and, if necessary, wash them. Put them some distance from the fire or in a slow oven or in the sun till dry and crisp, but not brown. Pull all the leaves off, and rub them through a coarse sieve, and bottle for use, or tie in bunches by the stems, and hang up till dry; then put in paper bag for use.

Mushrooms may be dried slowly in same way and rubbed through sieve. Excellent for adding to soups and stews.

How to Gather and Keep (2)

Roots ought to be dug in the fall after the roots and leaves are dead or have come to maturity; or, they should be dug before they start in the spring. They ought to be washed immediately after they are dug, or not washed at all. Some roots are injured by being put into water, especially those of an aromatic nature. All roots, when cleaned, ought to be put in a place where they will dry soon. They should not be placed in the sun but in a dry apartment where, they will be placed under the influence of fire heat, as on an upper floor while fire is kept below. As soon as they are perfectly dry they ought to be packed away and kept from the air as much as possible.

How to Gather and Keep (3)

Just before or while the herbs are in blossom gather them on a dry day, tie in bundles and hang up with the blossoms downward. When they are perfectly dry those that are to be used as medicine should be wrapped in paper and kept from the air while those that are to be used in cooking should have the leaves picked off, pounded, sifted fine and corked tightly in bottles.

How to Use Herbs

Teas or Infusions are made by pouring boiling water on the plant or bark and allowing it to steep for a short time until the water cools, after which the liquid is strained. Sometimes cold water is used. Infusions are made by steeping like tea. The infusion is generally better than the decoction as boiling destroys the virtue of some herbs. Usually, from 1 to 4 ounces of the herb should be used to a pint of boiling water.

Decoctions are solutions made by boiling the herbs in water and straining while hot. Decoctions are made by boiling like coffee.

Cerates are ointments containing 30 parts of beeswax to 70 parts of lanolin or some other substance to make them harder for use. They are used for piles, etc. Cerates are slower to dissolve when used where you do not desire a quick dissolving of the lanolin or other base.

Ointments are made without beeswax and are softer than cerates and are good for local application. The base is vaseline or lanolin (sheep's oil). The medicine is rubbed into the base. Ointments dissolve readily.

Extracts are made by taking the soluble parts from the plant. This is done by allowing them to stand in water or alcohol. Extracts consist of the soluble parts of plants reduced to a semi-solid condition by evaporation.

Fluid Extracts are made in the same way as solid extracts except that they are not so completely evaporated.

Syrups are solutions of sugar in water or sometimes in gummy substances. To make a syrup of plants, add simple syrup to the infusion when hot and somewhat evaporated and then bottle while hot. In other words, first make a tea of the plant and then add sugar.

Powders or dried herbs are finely broken up or pulverized to make powders.

Tinctures are solutions of the medical properties of herbs in alcohol or in mixtures of alcohol and water. Take the fresh or dried herb, chop and pound, and to 1 ounce of the herb add 2 ounces of alcohol. Allow the mixture to stand in a bottle from 8 to 14 days in a cool place. Then turn off the liquid carefully and bottle for use.

Fomentations are plants applied locally in infusion or decoction. Put the herbs into a bag and steep and then wring the bag out of the liquid and apply hot. This will hold heat longer than cloths. Fomentations are bags of herbs wrung out of the hot herb teas and applied to the affected parts.

Liniments are made with oily substances often mixed with powerful drugs.

Remedies

Arbor Vitae

An ointment made of the branchlets and cones is excellent for rheumatism. Make a poultice by powdering the cones and mixing with milk and it will cure the worst rheumatic pains. A decoction made of the branchlets or roots is good for coughs, ague, fevers and scurvy.

Arbor Vitae

To remove warts rub frequently with the gum from the arbor vitae tree.

Asparagus

May be used either as a tea or in decoction by using 2 ounces of the plant to a pint of water. Take from ½ to 1 teaspoonful 5 times a day. Asparagus tea is good for dropsy. It is used as a diuretic and heart sedative.

Asparagus purifies the blood.

Baking Soda

Dissolve enough common baking soda in water to make it thick, rub on the wart as often as you please and it will soon disappear. A lady living in Birmingham, Alabama, writes, "I have seen this tried many times and always with success."

An Indian storage building in a Canyon of Logy Creek, Yakima Indian Reservation, Washington. Photo taken August 27, 1917. *Courtesy of the Washington State University Library, L. V. McWhorter Collection*

Ashes and Vinegar

Burn some common willow bark, mix the ashes with strong vinegar and apply frequently to wart.

Barberry

It is a tonic and diuretic and is especially good for kidney troubles, cloudy urine, diminished urine, pain in passing urine and pain in back and front. It is also good for gravel. The tea is made from the bark of the stem and root and the dose is from 1 to 4 teaspoonfuls 4 times a day. The dose of the fluid extract is from 10 to 30 drops 3 or 4 times a day. The tea is made by using from 1 to 2 ounces of the bark to a pint of boiling water.

Bayberry

The bark is the part used and is made into a tea, decoction, or tincture. Use 1 to 4 ounces of tea for kidney and bladder trouble.

Bearberry

Particularly for kidney, bladder and urinary passages. In making the decoction use an ounce of the leaves to 1½ pints of water and boil down to a pint. The dose is from ½ to 3 ounces or half a small glassful 3 or 4 times a day. The dose of the powder is from 5 to 10 grains and of the fluid extract from ½ to 1 dram.

Beeswax and Sweet Oil

Dissolve a small piece of beeswax in a little sweet oil. Two or three applications while warm will effect a cure for chapping.

Blackberry-Red Raspberry-Dewberry

The leaves and bark of the root are the parts used. Boil the bark in milk and it is good for dysentery when taken freely. Or, a very valuable preparation for dysentery is to take 2 pounds of bruised unripe blackberries and simmer them with 1 pound of loaf sugar and ½ pint of brandy. A decoction made of the bark of blackberry and dewberry is good for use in diarrhea, dysentery, cholera infantum, relaxed condition of the bowels in children and slow bleeding from the stomach and bowels.

Beets and Turnips

Beets and turnips are excellent appetisers.

Blue Violet

A decoction made of this plant is valuable in the treatment of eruptive diseases of children and a syrup made of the petals is excellent for sore throat, coughs and constipation of children.

Boracic Acid

Sprinkle boracic acid in the shoes for either corns or foot sweating.

Borax and Camphor

Take a quart of boiling water; add an ounce of pulverized borax and half an ounce of powdered camphor; apply once a week with a sponge or flannel and it will prevent the falling hair.

Boxwood (Not Dogwood)

The bark steeped and drank is a splendid remedy for menstrual troubles, especially in young girls. It was extensively and successfully used for this purpose by the early settlers. Drink freely of the tea made of the bark.

Bran

When a light but thick poultice is required, bran should be boiled in water and placed in a bag and tied tightly. Press out the surplus water and apply to the parts. Cover well as it cools quickly.

Cabbage

Cabbage leaves are a good application for chilblains. Either alum water or turpentine is good as a wash. If the parts are unbroken either tincture of capsicum or prepared paper of capsicum may be applied. A salve made of rosin and ichthyol ointment is good. Iodine and lard in equal parts will also give relief.

Camphor

For soft corns apply, 2 or 3 times daily, a piece of cotton wet with tincture of camphor and keep cotton between the toes until the corns have entirely disappeared.

Cinnamon Oil

Apply it several times a day for a week or more. A lady living at Garrettsville, Ohio, says she cured a seed wart with this. It must be used some time but will effect a cure.

Clay

Wet clay earth or black mud applied to bites and stings is one of the best remedies and one that is easily obtained.

Cloves

A decoction of cloves will relieve sickness at the stomach and to check vomiting and for wind colic. The decoction is made by boiling 2 or 3 teaspoonfuls of ground cloves in ½ pint of sweet milk. The dose is a tablespoonful every 15 to 30 minutes as hot as can be borne. The oil of cloves put upon cotton and placed in the cavity of a tooth is good for toothache.

Cloves and Allspice were favorite seasonings in the old fashioned kitchen. The Clove is the "nail-shaped" flower bud of a tropical Asian tree. Allspice are the flavorful and aromatic berries of an American tree. *Courtesy of the Seattle Historical Society*

Cayenne

To relieve pain, apply a cayenne cloth. Boil teaspoonful cayenne, ½ pint water, or ½ vinegar and water, or whole vinegar, according to sensitiveness of skin, 5 minutes, then infuse by side of fire in jelly-can for 3 hours; strain, and wring cloth out of this. Keep on all night. You never take cold after it, so may go out in the morning.

Cayenne Pepper

Taken in small doses internally brings warmth and stimulates digestion. It is good for delirium tremens and to check the vomiting of drunkards and to stimulate the nervous system of those who are trying to stop drinking. Tincture of capsicum is used in liniments for neuralgia, rheumatism, headache, flatulent colic, etc. The powder is frequently sprinkled over the surface of plasters. The dose of tincture of capsicum is from 5 to 30 drops well diluted.

Molasses, Sulphur, Cayenne Pepper and Sweet Cream

Take ⅓ cup of molasses, 1 large teaspoonful of sulphur, ¼ teaspoonful of cayenne pepper and 3 large spoonfuls of sweet cream. Take a little in the mouth and swallow slowly whenever the cough is troublesome.

Celery

Celery acts on nervous system, and is a cure for rheumatism and neuralgia.

Comfrey

Bruise the fresh root for an application for bruises, ruptures, fresh wounds, sore breasts, ulcers, gout, etc. A decoction made by using from ½ to 2 ounces of the root to a quart of water is good for internal injuries. Drink the decoction freely during the day.

Corn Meal Poultice

This poultice is made by cooking corn meal in hot water until it sticks together. Apply to the seat of the pain as hot as it can be borne.

Chamomile

Good for colic and green diarrhea of babies. Make a tea by putting the flowers into cold water and give freely. Use 4 drams of the plant to a pint of cold water and give from 1 to 2 ounces at a dose. Chamomile makes good bitters for the stomach and is good for vomiting during pregnancy.

Chammomilla Tea

When hoarseness occurs in children and is attended with rough, dry cough, mucus and soreness in the throat and with fever in the evening, give chammomilla tea every 4 or 6 hours. Use no extenal application but pay proper attention to warmth and strictly avoid a variable temperature or humid atmosphere.

Chestnut

Chestnut leaf tea made from the green leaves and drank freely is good for whooping cough. The fluid extract is better for diarrhea. The dose is from 1 to 2 teaspoonfuls. The tea is made by using a handful of the leaves to a pint of water and the dose for children is ½ ounce 3 or 4 times a day.

Cinnamon

Cinnamon will stimulate and warm the stomach. It is good for bowel complaints. It is better known as a flavoring extract and to disguise the taste and smell of other medicines. The dose of cinnamon in powder is ⅓ of a small teaspoonful.

Catnip

This is a very good remedy for colds to produce sweating and also for colds and flatulence in babies. It is used warm. It is also very good to put into poultices. To make the tea use an ounce of the dried herb to a pint of water. This may be given freely to adults and to babies you can give from ¼ to ½ teaspoonful. It is a tonic when used cold. It is good for amenorrhea and dysmenorrhea and also for nervous headaches and irritability. One teaspoon at a dose of equal parts of fluid extract of catnip, fluid extract of valerian and fluid extract of skullcap, is very good for nervous headache, restlessness, etc. The leaves are used for poultices and also in fomentations for inflammations.

Caraway

It is good to relieve gas on the stomach. The tea is made by adding 2 teaspoonfuls of the seeds to a pint of boiling water. Do not boil tea. This tea may be taken freely. The dose of the oil is from 1 to 2 days. This is very good for wind colic in children.

Carrots

Carrots are good for asthma.

Cranberry

Bruise the desired quantity of cranberries and apply to the throat for quinsy and to swollen glands in scarlet fever and other diseases. Also fine for erysipelas. It gives relief in a few hours.

Cream

Cold fresh cream frequently applied will remove sunburn.

Dandelion

Make a decoction from the green plant for liver complaint, constipation, jaundice, dyspepsia, dropsy, blood purifier. The dose of the decoction is from 1 to 2 ounces taken frequently. Dandelion may be taken as a tea, the dried roots may be eaten or the plant may be eaten in the form of greens for either liver or bowl difficulties.

Elder Flower Tea and Cologne

Put a few drops of cologne into some elder flower tea and bathe the face for sunburn.

Flaxseed

While water is boiling add flaxseed to it very slowly until it becomes as thick as porridge. Continue the heat with constant stirring for 10 minutes. To make a poultice, spread on cotton and cover with gauze or cheese cloth which makes the covering next to the skin. Cover the whole with silk or flannel to retain the heat and if necessary, bandage snugly to keep it from slipping. Renew when cool.

Flaxseed Oil, Honey, and Whiskey

Equal parts of honey, flaxseed oil and whiskey; mix, and give a teaspoonful as the cough requires.

Flaxseed Tea

Steep ½ ounce of unbruised flaxseed in ½ pint of boiling water. Fine for coughs.

Freshair

Breathe plenty of fresh air, and you will be as well as God intended you should be.

Garlic

Take garlic juice. The dose is half a dram. This is also good for nervous and spasmodic coughs in children. The bruised bulbs, applied as a poultice on the chest and spine, are very good for children with pneumonia.

Garlic

It is an antiseptic and stimulating expectorant. It is good for coughs and colds. A poultice of garlic is good for croup. It is very good in chronic bronchitis and in capillary bronchitis of children. Garlic is generally used in syrup form. The dose is from 1/6 to 1 teaspoonful. Applied to the feet it is fine for convulsions of children. The dose of the fresh juice of the bulb is from ½ to 1 teaspoonful. Avoid overuse. It causes headache, flatulence, stomach disturbance, piles and fever.

Ginger

Powdered or bruised ginger is made into a tea, tincture and spice poultice. The dose of tincture of ginger is from 10 drops to a teaspoonful. For a child with colic or diarrhea give from 1 to 4 drops every 2 hours.

Ginseng

The root may be tinctured, made into a decoction or tea. The root may be tinctured in old Jamaica spirits and taken 3 times a day on an empty stomach. Good for pain in the bones from colds, devility, weakness from excessive venery, gravel and is a good restorative.

Golden Rod

Using sweet scented golden rod, the tea should not be boiled. Given freely while warm it is good for nausea or sickness at the stomach.

Hog's Lard

Chapped hands can generally be cured by keeping clean and applying hog's lard. Keeping the hands clean is a good preventive and especially with children.

Ginger is the pungent root of a tropical plant much used by early homemakers to add zest to molasses cakes such as gingerbread and as a flavoring for brews and beverages. *Courtesy of the Seattle Historical Society*

Hollyhock

A tea made of flowers may be drank freely and is fine for leucorrhea. It is also used for inflammation of the mucous surfaces.

Honey and Vinegar

A little in the mouth every little while for coughs and hoarseness.

Hop Tea

Take a good handful of hops, 20 camomile flowers and 10 cloves. Pour over them 1 quart boiling water; let it stand 12 hours. Strain, and drink ⅓ of a teacupful at a time. If it agrees with you, can take it three times a day.

Hops

Hop pillows, which can be had from a chemist, are also good. They can be used as a tea or a tincture. The tea is made by using a handful of hops to a quart of water. The dose of the tea is from 2 to 5 ounces. The smaller dose is to be taken as a tonic and the larger as a sedative.

Horehound

Horehound is generally given as a tea or a syrup for coughs, cold and lung troubles.

Horehound Candy

Dissolve about two sticks of horehound candy in half a cup of boiling water and drink while hot before going to bed.

Horseradish, Vinegar, Honey

Take 4 ounces of grated fresh horseradish and let it stand in a pint of good vinegar over night, then add a pint of honey and bring it to the boiling point, then strain and squeeze out. Take 1 or 2 teaspoonfuls several times a day. Very good for hoarseness, loss of voice and all ordinary coughs.

Indian Turnips

The root is the only part used. The fresh roots are too caustic to be used internally. They must be used in substance with milk, honey or molasses. May be taken 3 times a day for colds, coughs, etc.

Lemon

Small doses of the juice have a stimulating effect upon the stomach and aid digestion. An excellent drink for allaying thirst is made by using the juice of one lemon to a pint of water and sweetening with sugar. Hot lemonade is valuable for producing sweating and breaking up colds. As a wash the juice is good for removing tan from the face and hands.

Lemon

Drink freely of lemon juice mixed with sugar for hiccoughs.

Lemon

To remove corns try binding on a piece of lemon at night and leaving until morning. Two or three applications are all that are needed.

Lemon

Bathe the feet in hot water and drink a teacupful of hot lemonade before going to bed for a cold.

Lemon

Take hot lemonade just before going to bed. This is an old and tried remedy for a cold.

Lemon

One-half lemon in each glass to the extent of three lemons a day, then increase to six lemons a day and continue using until rheumatism, colds, heart-trouble, facial neuralgia, lumbago and kindred ailments disappear. Then reduce to two lemons daily. Use no starches, few proteins (better use none at all for several weeks), eat quantities of greens, cabbage, lettuce and all fresh vegetables, cooked or raw, large quantities of fruit, especially oranges, no tea or coffee, however weak, no sugar, preserves, jelly, jam, cake or pie.

Lettuce

Lettuce is good for relieving the pain of colic and of chronic rheumatism and is also good for coughs and diarrhea. Lactucarium is a preparation made from the juice and the dose is from 3 to 5 grains.

Lettuce and Cucumbers

Lettuce and cucumbers have a cooling effect on the system, and lettuce is good for sleeplessness.

Lycopodium

To relieve chapping, mix 2 drams of lycopodium with 3 drams each of subnitrate of bismuth and zinc oleate. Apply 3 times a day to hands or cheeks that are chapped from exposure to cold or wet. Cold cream and camphor are also very good.

Mix 2 drams each of pulverized calamine and pulverized zinc oxide with 4 drams of glycerine, 2 ounces of alcohol and enough water to make a pint. This is for chafing of infants. Apply with a soft cloth after each removal of the diaper and allow to dry. This is good where there is diarrhea and irritating urine.

Marigold

For cuts and wounds in either man or beast. An infusion may be made by using about 2 ounces of the leaves and flowers to a pint of boiling water. This is for extenal use only.

Milk and Red Pepper

For hoarseness take milk and red pepper every little while.

Milkweed

Bruise milkweeds and apply the milk that runs from them to the warts several times a day and they will soon come off.

Musk

Hiccoughs are caused by a spasmodic contraction of the diaphragm by which the air is suddenly drawn in. Give a 1 dram dose of tincture of musk. Another remedy is composed of spirits of camphor, 1 teaspoonful; tincture of capsicum, 2 or 3 drops; oil of amber, 5 to 10 drops; tincture of valerian, 1 teaspoonful. The whole is to be taken at a dose and repeated if necessary.

Milkweed

Milkweed is good for dropsy, catarrh, rheumatism and sores. To make a decoction, boil from 4 to 8 ounces of the dried root in 6 quarts of rain water. Take from 2 to 4 ounces at a dose 4 times a day for dropsy and rheumatic affections.

Mustard

This is a warm stimulating medicine when something is needed to liven the stomach. A poultice made with mustard alone or with horseradish leaves mixed with vinegar, bread crumbs and white of eggs, makes a fine application for neuralgia, but do not leave on long enough to blister. Mustard applied locally is good for pains almost anywhere.

Mustard Plaster

Take a piece of brown paper the size required, and a piece of muslin the same size. Mix into a paste as much mustard as will be required to cover the paper; spread evenly, cover with muslin, and turn over the edges of the paper about ½ inch; keep the plaster in position with a binder. When removed, wash part gently with soap and water, put on cotton wool, and replace the binder.

Mutton Suet

Mutton suet is an excellent remedy for dry lips and chapped hands. Render it down, run into cakes, and use nightly. If you use M'Clinton's Barilla Ash Soap, and dry the hands well, they will never chap. It is made from the ash of plants, and its mildness makes it par excellence a toilet soap. If the hands have become chapped, fill a pair of old loose kid gloves with well-wrought lather of this soap, putting these on just when getting into bed, and wearing till morning. Doing this for two or three nights will cure chapped, or even the more painful "hacked," hands, where the outer skin has got hard and cracked down to the tender inner layer.

Mustard Lotion

Mix 2 oz. mustard with ½ pint spirits of wine and 2 drachms of camphor; let it stand 3 days in a bottle carefully corked, then strain it off, and keep closely bottled for use. It is excellent for sprains, rheumatism, etc.

Nutmeg, Alum, Cloves, Etc.

To relieve nightsweats: Take one good-sized nutmeg, a lump of alum of the same size and a teaspoonful of cloves; pulverize all and add to half a pint of brandy or good whiskey. Dose: a tablespoonful 3 times a day, shaking well each time before using.

Olive Oil

Rub a little olive oil into the scalp every 4 to 5 days to cure baldness.

Onion

Rub the bald parts of the head with an onion to stimulate growth of new hair.

Onion

For bites and stings apply a piece of raw onion to the wound. Change the piece of onion every ten minutes and relief will soon be obtained. One physician says he uses no other remedy.

Onion

Onion can be used as an expectorant or poultice. When used as a poultice they are very fine for croup, laryngitis and earache. Added to sugar and water they are good as a cough syrup.

Onions

Onions, garlic, leeks, olives, shallots all possess medicinal virtues of a marked character, stimulating the circulatory system, and giving consequent increase of saliva and gastric juice, promoting digestion.

Onion Juice and Sugar

Take a good-sized onion and bake in a hot oven, press out the juice, mix with sugar, and take a little of it every few minutes. A lady in Ohio says she has frequently tried this for coughs and hoarseness with good results and many others all over the country can say the same thing.

Parsley

A poultice can be made from the crushed leaves. The fresh root is best for the tea by using an ounce of the root to a pint of water and the dose is from ½ to 2 ounces taken hot. Good for dropsy following scarlet fever and other eruptive diseases. The dose is ½ ounce every 2 to 4 hours. The seeds and leaves sprinkled on the hair will destroy vermin. Fomentations of the leaves are applied for bites and stings of insects.

Peroxide/Vinegar

For stings of hornets or bees pull out the sting and apply peroxide of hydrogen. Vinegar either pure or dilluted is good. Apply a mud poultice made of clay. For mosquito bites apply phenol, one part, mixed with water from 50 to 100 parts.

Potatoes and Salt

Slice some raw potatoes, leaving the skins on; sprinkle a little salt over them and wash the chilblains with the liquid that settles in the bottom of the dish.

Potato Skins

Place the inside of the skin of a boiled potato to the corn and let it remain for 12 hours to remove.

Pumpkin Seed

Eat a lot of the shelled seeds at night to rid of tapeworms. Follow in the morning with rochelle salts and castor oil. Pumpkin seeds are one of the very best remedies known for expelling tapeworms. They are also good for suppression of the urine.

Putting hops in a barn in the Ole Lee farm near Conway in Skagit County, Washington. *Courtesy of the Seattle Historical Society*

Peppermint

It is useful to ease the distress of nausea and vomiting, to relieve hysterics and to prevent the griping effects of cathertics and colic in children. The tea is made by using an ounce of the herb to a quart of boiling water. The dose is from 1 dram to 1 ounce and may be taken frequently. The dose of essence for an adult is from 5 to 6 drops in hot sweetened water. The dose of oil of peppermint is from 1 to 5 drops in hot water.

Peppermint, Oil Of

A little oil of peppermint rubbed over a sensitive corn relieves the soreness in a remarkable way.

Peppermint or Spearmint Tea

Warm peppermint or spearmint tea is an old tried remedy for wind on the stomach.

Quince Seeds, Borax and Glycerine

To 12 ounces of warm water add ½ ounce of quince seed, let stand for several hours until thick, and strain. Dissolve ¼ ounce of powdered borax in a little of this mixture and stir in with the rest. Add 2 ounces of glycerine and any perfume desired. This is excellent for softening the hands.

Quince Seed, Glycerine, Alcohol, Etc.

Mix 4 ounces of rain water, 4 ounces of rose water, 2 ounces of glycerine, 1 ounce of alcohol, ½ ounce of quince seed and 2 grains of morphine. A lady living at McKees Rocks, Pa., says she has used this for years and knows of nothing to compare with it.

Raisin Tea

May be infused like tea, or cook ½ pound raisins split and stoned, and 1 pint boiling water rather slowly for about 2 hours, strain and take hot or cold. A good mild laxative, one often used after abdominal operations, 5 oz. being given every 4 hours. Alternating with milk, 5 oz. every 4 hours.

Red Clover

For the tea use a handful of clover tops to a pint of water and give 1 or 2 drams at a dose. Taken frequently it is good for whooping cough. Taken alone or in combination it is also good for blood diseases such as scrofula, chronic rheumatism and skin diseases. A syrup is also made and used internally. May be taken freely. Good for sores and ulcers when freely applied.

Rhubarb

Mix thoroughly 2 ounces of powdered rhubarb, a pound of magnesia and an ounce of pulverized ginger. Keep in air tight bottles. This is a standard remedy used by physicians for bowel complaints of children. The rhubarb moves the irritating material from the bowels and the ginger stimulates the membrane to action.

Rhubarb

Roast, but do not burn, some powdered rhubarb and put 1 ounce into a pint of brandy or blackberry wine with enough essence of cinnamon to give it a good flavor and then sweeten with loaf sugar. A teaspoonful or more for children is a very good remedy in bowel complaints.

Saffron

To bring out the eruption of measles, scarlet fever and other eruptive diseases, make a saffron tea from the flowers. Gives tone to the stomach and is also good for spasms.

Sage

A tea is made by using from 4 to 8 ounces of sage to a pint of boiling water and the dose is from 1 ounce to a wineglassful for a tonic, astringent and stimulant. Good for summer complaints and worms in children. For colds and checking the night sweats of tuberculosis.

Sage Tea, Honey, and Vinegar

Take 1 tablespoonful of honey, 2 tablespoonfuls of vinegar and enough sage tea to make half a pint. Use as a gargle for tonsilitis and quinsy.

Sage Tea

To relieve nightsweats, drink freely of cold sage tea. The warm sponge bath should be used at night and cold sponging of the body in the morning on rising. Wipe dry each time and make use of severe friction or rubbing with a coarse dry towel.

Sage Tea

Make some sage tea and rub on the scalp every night for one week; then wash the hair and repeat. This may grow hair as well as prevent its falling.

Salt

For chilblains, once a week bathe the feet and hands in hot salt water. This is both a preventive and a cure.

Salt added to the bath is a cleanser and it also beautifies and strengthens.

Salt

Salt will remove tartar from the teeth. Mixed with equal parts of soda it makes a good tooth powder.

Salt

A strong solution of salt and water is excellent for hardening sensitive gums.

Salt-Soda

Table salt and baking soda, in equal parts, applied to spider bites will relieve the pain and stop the swelling.

Sarsaparilla

For chronic rheumatism, syphilis, scrofula and chronic skin diseases and to cleanse the blood, make a compound decoction of sarsaparilla. Take 10 parts of sarsaparilla, 2 parts sassafras, 2 parts guaiac wood, 2 parts of licorice root, 1 part of leatherwood and 83 parts of water. The dose is from 1 to 4 ounces.

Sloe Jam

Requires 1 pound sugar to 1 pound fruit, and is made like gooseberry jam. Excellent for colds.

Sassafras

Make a tea of wood, root and bark. Use 1 ounce of sassafras to a pint of water. The dose is from 2 drams to an ounce. The dose of oil of sassafras is from 1 to 4 drops. The tea is good for rheumatism, and for kidney troubles.

Spearmint

Good for nausea and vomiting. Good for gravel, suppressed urine and painful urination. Crush the green plant and add enough Holland gin to make a saturated tincture. Take a wineglassful as often as you can possibly bear it for suppressed urine and gravel.

SAFFLOWER.—(*Carthamus tinctorius.*)

Courtesy of the Seattle Historical Society

Spices

Spices make a good poultice. Mix equal parts of ground cinnamon, cloves, allspice and ginger and if you wish to have it very strong you can add ¼ part of cayenne pepper. Place this in a flannel bag and spread evenly and wet with alcohol or whiskey before applying. This will last for a long time by rewetting. It is fine for pains in the abdomen.

Spinach

Spinach has a direct effect on the kidneys; and dandelions, cooked as greens, have the same.

Starch

Moisten some powdered starch and rub on the parts to stop the itching.

Strawberry

Strawberries are a very valuable remedy for either kidney or bladder troubles. Strawberry leaf tea with alum is good for sore mouth.

Strawberries

Rub crushed strawberries over the face at night for sunburn.

Sumach

A tea made from sumach berries and sweetened with honey is good for sore throat when used as a gargle. If sweetened with loaf sugar it is good for dysentery, diarrhea and other bowel complaints. For old sores and ulcers a splendid poultice may be made from either the berries or the bark. Either the fluid extract or the decoction will relieve kidney troubles and especially where there is suppression of incontinence of kidney troubles. From 10 to 30 drops of the fluid extract may be taken during each day.

Sunflower

The seeds and leaves of the sunflower can be used as a diuretic and expectorant and have been used in kidney, throat and lung affections. Put 2 pounds of the bruised seeds into 5 gallons of water and boil down to 3 gallons, strain, add 12 pounds of sugar and 1½ gallons of good Holland gin. The dose of this is from 2 drams to 2 ounces 3 or 4 times a day.

A harbinger of spring was the yearly dose of tonic to purify the blood. Whether it be a dose of castor oil, mother's special concoction or sarsaparilla. This old trade card calls attention to Ayer's Sarsaprilla. *Courtesy of the Seattle Historical Society*

Sunflower Seeds, Gin and Sugar

Put two pounds of bruised sunflower seeds into 5 gallons of water, boil down to 3 gallons, strain, and add 12 pounds of sugar and 1½ gallons of Holland gin. The dose is from 2 drams to 2 ounces 3 or 4 times a day or oftener for a cough, tickling in the throat, etc.

Sweet Clover

A tea is made of the leaves and flowers for coughs and leucorrhea. It is most frequently used as a poultice or an ointment for swellings and inflammations.

Sweet Clover Ointment

Stew some sweet clover in lard and add equal parts of beeswax and white pine turpentine until it forms an ointment of the proper consistency. A fine ointment for general purposes.

Thyme

Oil of thyme contains thymol which is a valuable antiseptic. A tea can be made of the plant and is good as an injection for leucorrhea. It is good in very small doses of from 1 to 2 drams as an intestinal antiseptic. Warm tea is good for hysteria, flatulence, colic and to produce sweating. In making the tea use an ounce of the plant to a pint of cold or hot water. The dose is from 1 to 3 ounces.

Tomatoes

Tomatoes act on the liver, and are a remedy for dyspepsia and indigestion.

Treacle

A simple and efficacious remedy for burns, scalds, and insect bites is always at hand, but not sufficiently known. It is treacle. If the burn be on the extremities, take a sufficient quantity of treacle to plunge the affected part in it. Where this is not practicable, apply a piece of cotton wool saturated in the syrup to the burn, and tie it over loosely with a bandage. Treacle is molasses, especially that which is a by-product of sugar refining. A medicinal compound of various ingredients, formerly believed to be capable of curing or preventing the effects of poison, especially that of a snake.

Turnips

Turnips are particularly good for chest complaints.

Watercress

Watercress is good for scurvy.

Wild Cherry Bark and Loaf Sugar

Put ten cents worth of wild cherry bark into a quart of water and boil down to a pint; add a pound of loaf sugar, strain and take a teaspoonful every half hour. This is fine for coughs.

Wild Cherry Syrup

Syrup of wild cherry is very good. This is for coughing and hoarseness.

Wintergreen

Essence or oil of wintergreen may be used or a tea may be made of the green plant. The tea is good to restore strength, promote menstruation and relieve asthma. The oil is used for neuralgia and rheumatism as it contains salicylic acid. The plant is a cordial, stimulant, restorative and partial antiseptic. It is excellent for some forms of chronic diarrhea. The dose of the oil of wintergreen is from 5 to 10 drops every 3 to 6 hours and this dose should be gradually increased until it causes ringing in the ears.

Witch Hazel

Witch hazel twigs and flowers are good in decoction. The bark can be used as a poultice for ulcers, piles, painful swellings, sprains and bruises. The tea of the leaves, one ounce to a pint of water, is good for sore eyes. A strong decoction of the leaves is good as an injection for falling womb and for piles and is also an excellent application for enlarged veins.

Wood Charcoal

Cut and split finely white or soft maple. Set in a small coal pit and when well burned take it out and put a small quantity at a time into an iron kettle. Pound fine and sift through a common sieve. Then put the whole into an iron kettle over the fire and heat until red hot and the coal ceases to send out a smoke. When cool, put into bottles and cork tightly.

Mix well with yeast and use as a poultice. For gas dyspepsia, indigestion, acid stomach and foul breath, give from a teaspoonful to a tablespoonful either before or after meals.

Early day drug stores such as this one of the 1880s were the source of herbs, tinctures and medications from which families were able to concoct liniments, salves, hair and clothes dye, perfume and toilet articles. Where no such facilities were available, they relied on garden produce and native wild plants for remedies and coloring. *Courtesy of the Seattle Historical Society*

REMINDERS

Cooking

Butter: To keep butter firm, put it in a basin and stand basin inside a larger one containing cold water. Cover all with damp cloth. Notice occasionally if cloth is getting dry, and if necessary, wet it again.

Butter: To cut butter into small even squares for the table, use a coarse wet thread, as this leaves no ragged edges.

Cake: Often a large slice has to be cut off the top of a cake to make it level for icing. An excellent way to prevent this waste is when putting the batter into the cake-tin to keep it up all round the sides, making quite a hole in the middle. Put in a nice hot oven, and as the cake always rises in the middle, it will, by the time it is cooked, have a nice flat surface.

Canning: When preparing cherries, plums, or crab apples for canning or preserving, the stem or a part of it may be left on the fruit.

Canning: If the peaches are to be canned in sirup, put them at once into the sterilized jars. They may be canned whole or in halves. If in halves, remove nearly all the stones or pits. For the sake of the flavor, a few stones should be put in each jar.

Corn-flour: A little corn flour added to the salt in the salt-cellar will prevent it hardening. ½ teaspoonful of corn-flour to 2 tablespoonfuls of salt will be enough. A pinch of salt added to mustard prevents it from souring.

Fat for Frying Doughnuts, Croquettes, Etc.: Fry out carefully 2½ pounds of beef suet, add 1 pound of fresh lard. After using, strain and put in small bucket and cover; may be used a number of times.

Larder: To keep a larder fresh, place a pan of charcoal in it, for it helps greatly to keep everything sweet and wholesome.

Lemon Juice: Lemon juice sprinkled over sliced fruit for dessert or over fruit in salad will prevent it turning dark.

Milk: To keep milk in hot weather: Boil all milk not to be used immediately, or it may get into that dangerous condition which is known as "on the turn." "Turned" milk is a very dangerous drink in hot weather, particularly for children.

Stoning Raisins: The simplest way to stone raisins is to pour hot water over the fruit and then drain, and proceed to stone the raisins in the usual way. If your meat-chopping machine seems dull, just grind a piece of scouring brick through the chopper and see how well it sharpens and polishes it.

Cleaning and Washing

Bottles: Discolorations, and green marks from vegetation, etc., may be removed from bottles thus—put into the bottle a raw potato cut into small pieces, with a tablespoonful of salt and twice that amount of water; shake well until the stains are removed, then rinse in clear water. Stains of all kinds may be removed by rinsing the bottles first with muriatic acid (spirits of salt) and afterwards with clear water.

Cretonne: Cretonne requires very careful washing, as there is danger of the colours running. Soak the material in cold water, with salt added, for a few hours first. Allow a handful of salt to a gallon of water. Then wash in tepid soapsuds, previously made by making a lather with boiled soap. Do not rub soap on the cretonne, simply pass it through two soapy waters, rubbing it gently with the hands until it is quite clean, then rinse in warm water, and afterwards in cold water. Iron on the wrong side. Be sure to avoid the use of soda or washing powders.

Furniture: Rub with equal proportions of linseed oil, turpentine, vinegar and spirits of wine. Shake well before using.

Mrs. Haley sewing on a treadle machine on May 14, 1913. *Courtesy of the Henderson Collection, Washington State University Library*

Furniture: Take a large jar, set it on the range, and shred 6 oz. bee's-wax and 2 oz. white wax, and 2 oz. castile soap into it. Stir till melted, and add 2 pints boiling water and 2 pints turpentine. Remove from the fire, and stir occasionally until it is quite cold, when it should be like a very thick cream. It can be kept in the jar, but if you have old pickle bottles it is better, to pour it into them while still warm, and occasionally stir until quite cold. It wil keep for years, and is better old than new.

Before polishing furniture, wash it with clean, cold water, and polish with new chamois leather. Oak or varnish paint, same way.

A very useful recipe for brightening up furniture is made of the following: 1 gill raw linseed oil, ½ gill turpentine. Mix well together. A duster, moistened with this, and a dry, soft cloth to finish, will make furniture shine like new.

Glass Decanter: Put into it a spoonful of vinegar and a few lumps of soda. Shake it well but leave the top open or it may burst the decanter. Rinse with cold water.

Gold Chains, Etc.: Let the article lay in a solution of caustic potash until all the dirt is removed.

Linoleum or Oil Cloth: Instead of using soap and water, wash with sweet milk. The milk makes it look fresh and bright without destroying the luster.

Mud on Clothing: Use a corn-cob to rub the mud from the clothing, then brush well.

Red Flannel: Wash in same manner as white, except to the last water add vitriol, in proportion of 1 teaspoonful to 3 gallons of water; this fixes the colour. Salt may be used, one large handful to about 2 gallons of water, but it has the drawback of making the flannel absorb moisture.

Home life. Woman washing clothes with Universal Clothes Wringer. *American Agriculturist, June 1861*

Stove Polish: Take black lead (plumbago), finely pulverized, and put into 2-ounce wooden boxes; label them neatly and retail for 10 or 15 cents per box, or wholesale at $6.00 per hundred. It costs three cents per box to prepare.

Directions—This polish requires no mixing which is so disagreeable to the housewife. Dip a damp woolen cloth into the box and apply to the stove, then polish with a dry cloth.

Spots: To remove tar, wagon grease, mixtures of fat, carbon and acetic acid on white goods apply soap and oil of turpentine, alternating with streams of water. If the spots are on colored cottons or woolens, rub in with lard; let it lie; soap; let lie; and proceed, alternating with oil of turpentine and water. Treat silks the same only use benzine in place of turpentine.

Wall Paper: Blow the dust off the wall with a bellows and then, beginning at the top of the room, go all over the paper, rubbing it with downward strokes with pieces of stale bread. Or, tie about two quarts of wheat bran in a flannel and go over the paper with that. Or, dry corn meal may be used instead of bread. Apply on a cloth. Grease spots may be removed by laying a blotter over them and then holding a hot flatiron on the blotter.

Washing Windows: Add a tablespoonful of either powdered borax or ammonia to a gallon of warm water and wash the windows, using a chamois to dry and polish them.

Mending

Cement: Mix litharge and glycerine until of the consistency of thick cream or fresh putty. This is good for fastening on lamp posts, mending stone jars, stopping leaks in seams of wash boilers or tin pans, cracks in iron kettles, etc. It is not affected by water, heat or acids.

China: Dissolve gum arabic in water until it is quite thick and then stir in plaster of Paris until it makes a sticky paste. Apply with a brush, stick the pieces together and after three days you cannot break the china in the same place.

Earthenware: Broken glass or earthenware can be easily mended by this simple recipe. Tie broken edges together so that they will stay in place. Do not wash or wet them after they are broken, but put them in a flat kettle and cover with skim milk. Put kettle on fire and let simmer for 2 hours or more. Then remove, and when cold take the ware out carefully and put it on one side for a month, when it will be ready for use.

Glue Substitute: Take a small piece of cold potato, which has been boiled, and rub it up and down a piece of paper with your fingers for about five minutes. It will become the right consistency and stick as well as the strongest glue.

Hot-Water Cans, Leaks In Stoves, Kettles, Or Iron Articles: Mix equal quantities of glycerine and litharge (oxide of lead) to the consistency of thick cream. It resists the action of hot or cold water, and almost any degree of heat. Only mix a little at a time, very thick, more like putty than cream. Let the article when mended harden for a week before using.

Iron Vessels: Mix finely some sifted lime with the white of an egg till a thin paste is formed, then add some iron filings. Apply this to the fracture and the vessel will be found nearly as sound as ever.

Pests

Red Ants: Scatter sweet fern in the places they frequent.

Flies: Make flypaper by melting together 1 oz. resin, 1 oz. castor oil, add a few drops honey and a small piece bee's-wax, and spread on firm papers. Try a little first, to see if proper consistency, when cool. If not hard enough, add a trifle more resin.

Mice: Mice do not like the smell of camphor gum and if it is placed in drawers or trunks they will keep at a distance. Seeds may also be protected by mixing small pieces of camphor gum with them.

Moths: Take 1 oz. of each of the following:—cloves, nutmeg, mace, caraway seeds, cinnamon and Tonquin beans, and 6 oz. orris-root; grind to a powder, mix thoroughly, and put in muslin bags, which store amongst your clothes. Besides imparting a delicious fragrance, these help to keep away moths. Or place lumps of naphthaline, or whole cloves, among your blankets or furs, etc.

Moths: Camphor gum is a preventive of moths. Goods packed in a cedar chest will be kept free from moths. Exposing clothes and furs occasionally to the light and air and beating and shaking them is probably the best treatment, however.

Rats: Scatter either sulphur or sage about the places they frequent and you will get rid of the troublesome pests.

Miscellaneous

Axle Grease: One pound tallow, ¼ pound black lead, ¼ pound castor oil; melt the tallow; add the other ingredients and rub all together until cold and well mixed.

Breakfast-Table Barometer: A cup of hot coffee is an unfailing barometer, if you allow a lump of sugar to drop to the bottom of the cup and watch the air bubbles arise without disturbing the coffee. If the bubbles collect in the middle, the weather will be fine; if they adhere to the cup, forming a ring, it will either rain or snow; and if the bubbles separate without assuming any fixed position, changeable weather may be expected.

Candles: To make candles last double time, take each by the wick and coat with white varnish. Dry and harden. The varnish forms a cup which holds the fat, and grease cannot run down to waste.

Candles: A candle may be made to fit any candlestick by dipping it in very hot water.

Corkscrew: A convenient substitute for a corkscrew when the latter is not at hand may be found in the use of a common screw, with an attached string to pull out the cork.

Cure Utensils: Iron pots should be boiled out first with wood ashes and cold water and then thoroughly washed. They are then ready for use. Griddles, skillets, waffle irons and iron gem pans should be greased and allowed to burn off once or twice before they are used for cooking.

Cut or Break Glass: File a notch in the edge of the glass at the place you wish to begin to break from; then put a red hot iron on the notch and draw it in the direction you wish the glass to break. If the iron be drawn slowly a crack will follow it. Another way is to hold the glass level under water and cut with a pair of shears.

Cure a Sheepskin: Rub skin well with 2 handfuls salt and ½ pound pounded alum. Take one half of skin first; roll it up and let it lie for three days. Take some chalk and spread it over, and rub well with a sandy stone. Repeat on remainder of skin with rest of salt and alum, etc. Nail it up on door of outhouse or airy place to dry thoroughly, and afterwards wash it with soap and tepid water.

Destroy Odor by Burning Lamp Wicks: Boil new lamp wicks in vinegar and then thoroughly dry them. There will then be no odor from them when burning.

Glass: New glass should never be used until treated so that it is rendered, as near as possible, unbreakable. Place tumblers, etc., in a large pan, pack them round with hay, and then fill with cold water. Add handful salt. Place the pot on the fire and then bring it slowly to boiling-point. Then remove from the fire, and stand it aside until cold.

Gummed Labels: If postage stamps, gummed labels, or jam-pot covers have become glued together, do not soak in water, but lay a thin paper over them and pass a hot iron over. They will then come apart easily, and the gum will be intact.

Home Cement: Mix 2 parts sand, 2 parts sifted ashes and 1 part wheat flour with enough water to make putty like mass.

Kindling Fires: Soak corn-cobs in kerosene oil; when needed put a cob in the stove, set fire to it and put on the fuel.

Petrify Wood: Mix equal parts of rock alum, gem salt, white vinegar, chalk and peebles powder; after the ebullition has caused throw any piece of wood or other porous substance into the solution and it will petrify.

Purify Cictern Water: Cistern water may be purified by hanging a bag of charcoal in the water.

Purify Water: A large spoonful of pulverized alum will purify a hogshead of water. It should be thoroughly stirred in and it will be very effective in killing microbes.

Remove the Smell of Onions from the Breath: Parsley, eaten with vinegar, will destroy the unpleasant breath caused by eating onions.

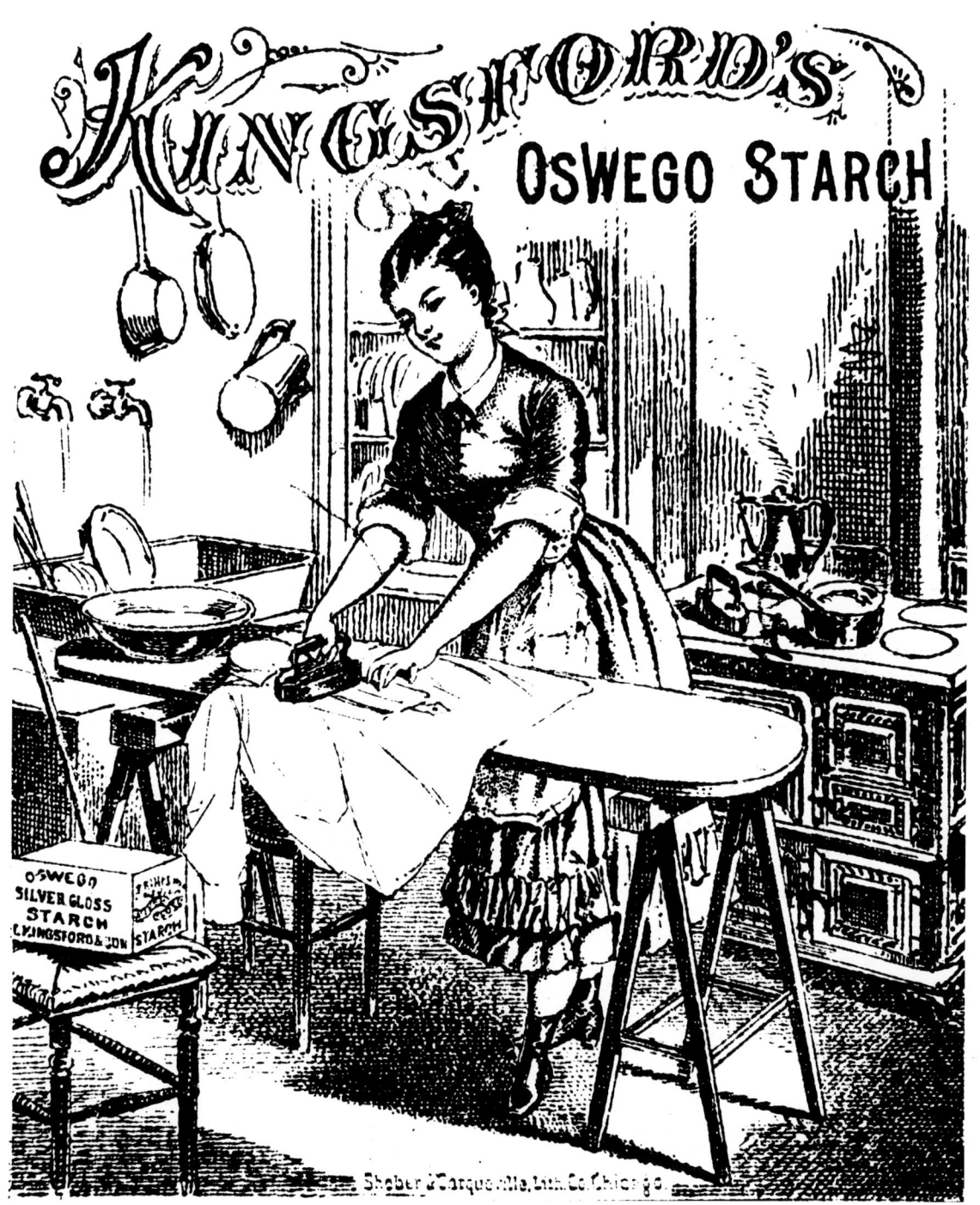

Today's doorstop was yesterday's sad iron and turn-of-the-century homemakers tested it for proper "sizzle" by applying a wet fingertip to the bottom of the iron when they removed it from a stovetop. *Courtesy of the Seattle Historical Society*

Render Children's Clothes Uninflammable: To 3 parts of dry starch add 1 part of tungstate of soda, and use in ordinary way. If material does not require starching dissolve 1 pound of the same in 2 gallons water. Well saturate the fabric and dry. Will not injure colour nor will ironing affect it.

1 oz. of alum added to rinsing water will make clothes practically uninflammable—would only smoulder very slowly, never burst into flame.

Sealed Well: Use large drill bit and drill down to and into solid rock. Then take a smaller bit, is attached and the hole carried on down to water. This leaves a shelf of solid rock. When well casing is put in it sits on that and round it is poured a composition consisting chiefly of coal tar. In that way the well is sealed and seepage kept out.

Saving Tainted Venison: Bury it in the ground in a clean cloth for a whole night and it will take away the corruption, savour and stink.

Saving Soap: Collect tiny morsels. Cut in thin shavings with old knife. Keep in old jar. When nearly full, pour cupful hot water over, set in pan of boiling water and stir till soap is entirely dissolved to about thickness of honey. Pour into tin box kept for purpose. Leave till quite cold, then bend back sides of box, when soap can be easily removed in nice firm block. Cut into neat pieces and keep in dry place.

A cake of hard soap rubbed in edge of drawers that will not run, will induce them to pull in and out easily.

The family of John Schultz photographed in July of 1911. Having a photograph taken was no small occasion. The family is shown in front of the farm buildings, their clothing is as fresh and clean as the washing airing on the clothes line in the background. The horses in the barnyard await another day's work in the expansive fields which stretch into the distance.

To Blacken Boots: Take a raw potato and cut in halves. Rub over boots well. Then rub blacking well in. Result will be so satisfactory it will be difficult to say boots were not always black.

To Curl Feathers: Wet them and when nearly dry draw each flue or fibre over the edge of a blunt knife, turning it the way you wnt it to curl; if the feather is to be flat, press it between the leaves of a book.

To Fluff Feathers: Sprinkle a little salt on a hot stove and hold the plume in the fumes for a few minutes.

To Dry Boots: Fill wet boots with dry oats and set aside for a few hours. The oats will draw the moisture from the boots and, swelling out, will keep the leather from shrinking and hardening as it would do if placed near the fire to dry.

To Prevent Hinges From Creaking: Dip a feather into oil and rub them with it.

To Prevent Mail From Being Read: A package or envelope sealed with white of egg cannot be steamed open.

To Remove Tight Rings: Thread a needle, flat in the eye, with a strong thread, pass the head of the needle with care under the ring, and pull the thread a few inches towards the hand. Wrap the long end of the thread tightly round the finger, regularly, all down towards the nail to reduce its size, then lay hold of the short end and unwind it. The thread repassing against the ring will gradually remove it from the finger. This never-failing method will remove the tightest ring without difficulty, however much swollen the finger may be.

To Save On Coal: Place a quantity of chalk in the grates. Once heated, this is practically inexhaustible from combustion, and gives out great heat. Place the chalk at the back of each of your fires in nearly equal proportions with the coal. Full satisfaction will be felt both as to the cheerfulness and as to the warmth of the fire, and the saving throughout the winter will be at the rate of 25 per cent.

Take old newspapers, about eight at a time, and roll them up as tightly as possible, binding the ends of the roll with wire to prevent it coming undone, and place on the fire. These rolls burn like coal, and give out a good heat. The wire can be used over and over again. To save coals, leave slide at top of range a little open; will have more heat and great saving of coals.

Whitewash: Add an ounce of carbolic acid to a gallon of whitewash or add copperas to ordinary whitewash until it is yellow. Copperas is a disinfectant and will drive away vermin. Carbolic acid will prevent the odors which taint milk and meat.

Whitewash: Dissolve five cents worth of glue in warm water and mix with ten cents worth of kalsomine, two quarts of soft soap and bluing. Fine for halls, fences, etc.

Writing Fluid: Rain water, one gallon; brown sugar, one-eighth pound; gum arabic, one-eighth pound; powdered nutgalls, three-eighth pound; clean copperas, one-eighth pound; bruise and mix, then let stand for 10 days, shaking occasionally; strain. If not used as a copying ink but one-fourth of the sugar or gum is needed as it will then flow more freely. This ink is fine for records and deeds for it may be read hundreds of years hence.

MISCELLANEOUS

Farmers' Standby

Wean calves or any nursing animal when the signs are in the knees or going down into the feet.

Plant all crops and vegetables that grow below the ground in the dark of the moon. Refer to your almanac for phases of the moon.

All grains and row crops that grow above the ground should be planted by the light of the moon.

Liniment, Salve and Toilet Receipts

Liniments

1) Mix equal parts of turpentine and coal oil and if for man add a little sweet oil to keep from blistering. This liniment is fine for all kinds of sprains, sores, swellings and frostbites.

2) To 2 quarts of raw linseed oil add 2 ounces of gum camphor and ½ ounce each of oils of cajeput and thyme and ¼ ounce each of oils of anise and wintergreen. The dose for a grown person is a teaspoon in a little water internally as often as required. Apply externally 3 or 4 times a day. Good also for bee stings.

3) Mix 2 ounces of spirits of camphor, 1 ounce of tincture of capsicum, ½ ounce of gum guaiac, ¼ ounce of gum myrrh and 3 ounces of alcohol.

4) To 1 quart of best alcohol add oils of hemlock and sassafras, spirits of turpentine, tincture of cayenne, guaiacum, catechu and laudanum, of each ½ ounce; tincture of myrrh, 2 ounces; oil of origanum and camphor gum, each 1 ounce; chloroform, ¾ ounce and oil of wintergreen, ¼ ounce. This is excellent for rheumatism, weak back, swellings, bruises, cuts, sprains and corns.

5) Into a pint bottle put ⅛ ounce of pulverized cayenne and 1 ounce of lobelia herb. Fill the bottle with whiskey and in 12 or 15 days it is ready for use. It is fine for cuts, bruises, sprains and strains in either man or beast.

6) Steep, but not boil, two teaspoonfuls of cayenne pepper in a teacupful of good vinegar, strain, and bottle for use. This will cause heat and is fine for rheumatism.

Salves and Plasters

1) Melt together 1 ounce of each of lard, rosin and beeswax; remove from the fire and when practically cool add 1 ounce of oil of spikenard.

2) Take 1 pound each of rosin beeswax and sheep's tallow and 1¼ pounds of raw linseed oil. Simmer down until of the proper consistency.

3) Simmer together ½ ounce of beeswax, 1 ounce of mutton tallow and 5 ounces of rosin. Make into rolls and when needed spread on a cloth and apply as hot as can be borne.

4) Slice a medium sized onion into 4 ounces of vaseline, stew together and strain. Apply two or three times a day to inflamed wounds.

Toilet Receipts

Cologne

To make a fragrant cologne combine two drachms oil of lavender, one drachm and a half of oil of rosemary, two drachms of essence of musk, one drachm each of oil of orange, lemon and bergamot, ten drops of attar of rose and a pint of proof spirit. Shake thoroughly three times a day for a week.

Beautiful needlework enhanced the clothing of this mother and her daughter who share a pleasant setting in an early 20th Century home. *Courtesy of the Washington State University Library, Henderson Collection*

Skin Refresher

Slice some cucumbers and let them stand in water for some time. Wash the face and hands with this water.

Hand Creams

1) Mutton tallow is good to soften hand. Rub it on when the hands are dry, the best time being upon going to bed. An old pair of gloves saturated on the inside with mutton tallow and glycerine in equal part, melted together, can be worn during the night with excellent results.

2) Thoroughly mix four parts of glycerine and five parts egg yolk to smooth the skin after having your hands in water.

To one ounce of glycerine and one ounce of alcohol add eight ounces of rose-water for chapped hands or face.

3) After washing the hands, rub in dry oatmeal.

4) Beeswax dissolved in a small quantity of sweet oil by heating carefully is good for chapped lips.

5) Indian meal and vinegar or lemon-juice will heal and soften roughened hands.

Hair Pomade

Take the marrow out of a bone and place it in warm water letting it come almost to the boiling point. Let it cool and pour the water away. Repeat three times. Beat the marrow to a cream with a silver fork and stir in half a pint of oil, drop by drop, beating continuously. When quite cold add ten cents' worth of citronella. Pour into jars and cover.

Hair Stimulant

Take a quarter of an ounce of chipped alkanet root, put in a bit of coarse muslin and place in a bottle containing eight ounces of sweet oil. Cover it to keep out the dust and let it stand several days. Then add to this sixty drops of cantharides, ten drops of oil of rose, and sixty each of neroli and lemon. Let it stand one week and you will have a stimulant for growth of hair.

Lotions

1) A mixture of glycerine, bay rum and rose water makes a good lotion. A few drops of bergamot added will give it a nice odor. Massage with the lotion while moist and dry with a towel.

2) Immediately after washing apply a mixture of rose oil and glycerine. It is good for the skin.

Cold Cream

Melt one ounce of oil of almonds, one-half ounce spermaceti, one drachm white wax and add two ounces of rose-water. Stir constantly until cold.

Perfumed Water

Add one quart of water and two ounces of proof spirit to twelve drops of attar of rose which has been rubbed together with half an ounce of white sugar and two drachms of carbonate magnesia. Filter through paper.

Wrinkle Cream

Melt and stir together one ounce of white wax, two ounces of strained honey and two ounces of juice of lily bulbs; apply to the face every night and it is said your wrinkles will disappear.

Making Soap and Lye

To Make Soap

To make boiled soft soap, put in a kettle all the grease that has accumulated such as the scraps and bones from the soup kettle, rinds of meat, etc.; fill the kettle half full. If there is too much grease it can be skimmed off after the soap is cold for another kettle of soap. This is the only sure test for enough grease in the soap, as the lye will consume all that is needed but no more. Make a fire under one side of it. The kettle should be out of doors. Let it heat very hot so as to fry; stir occasionally to prevent burning. Now put in the lye a gallon at a time, watching it closely until it boils, because it sometimes runs over. Add lye until the kettle is full enough but not so full that it can not boil well. Soap should boil from the side and not the middle as this is more likely to make it to boil over. To test the soap, to one spoonful of soap add one of rain water; if it stirs up very thick, the soap is good and will keep, but if it becomes thinner it is not good. This could be the fault of one of three causes, it is too weak, there is a deposit of dirt or it is too strong.

To Make Lye

Lye is made by perculating water and wood ashes. To set the leach for making lye, bore several holes in the bottom of a barrel; or use one without a bottom; prepare a board larger than the barrel, then set the barrel on it and cut a groove around just outside the barrel, making one groove from this to the edge of the board to carry off the lye as it runs off into the groove around it, running into one in the centre of the board. Place all two feet from the ground and tip so that the lye may run from the board into the vessel below prepared to receive it. Place half bricks or stones around the edge of the inside of the barrel; place on the bricks one end of some sticks about two inches wide, inclining them to the centre. On these place some straw to the depth of two inches and over it scatter two pounds of slaked lime. Put in ashes, about half of a bushel at a time, pack well by pounding down and continue to do this until the barrel is full, leaving a funnel-shaped hollow in the centre large enough to hold several quarts of water. Use rain water boiling hot. Let the water soak down before adding any more. If the ashes have been packed tightly, it may take two or three days before the lye will begin to run, but it will be all the stronger for it and much better. (Lye is extremely caustic and should be made, handled and kept with the most stringent care.)

Meaning of Flowers

Acacia Blossom: Come to my heart!
Alpine Rose: Love must venture; timidity will not win.
Anemone: My thought by day, my dream by night.
Anise: Mend your manners.
Apple Blossom: Who plucks the blossoms, destroys hopes of fruit.
Apricot Blossom: Are you always gay and trifling?
Aster: Weep no longer—you will find your love again above the stars.
Aspen Leaf: Your heart beats for all, therefore no heart beats for you.
Balsam Rose: Let me dwell in your heart.
Barley: Come again tomorrow.
Bean Blossom: Forgive me, I misunderstood you.
Blackberry Branch: Contentment and love.
Buckwheat Blossom: Not idle show, quiet, domestic virtues alone insure lasting happiness.
Burr: Like seeks like.
Buttercup: Your presence is consoling to me.
Cabbage Leaf: When you come again, come sober.
Carnation: How I burn!
Cherry Blossom: When will love tinge your cheeks?
Chestnut Blossom: Always as today.
Clover Blossom: I will live for you.
Columbine: Your words sound well, but what says your heart?
Daffodil: Let me not pine!
Dill: Love strengthens—I will protect you.
Fig Leaf: I am ashamed.
Flax: Do you love me for myself?
Grape Vine: Fear Not! Love conquers!
Honeysuckle: Eternal fidelity!
Iris: Why have you disturbed the peace of my heart?
Ivy: I am true.
Larkspur: Your love is my aim.
Lily-Tiger: My heart burns.
Lily-White: Let me adore you.
Marigold: I do not like you.
Nettle: Beware. Flirting has its penalty.
Peony: You are vain—of what?
Poppy: You are stupid.
Primrose: I will cherish your love.
Rose-Red: You are like a conqueror.
Rose-White: You are childlike in your innocence.
Rosebud: You fill me with longing.
Rose Petal-Red: Yes!
Rose Petal-White: No!
Sweet Pea: Your name is fickle!
Sweet William: Hasty impressions are soon effaced.
Thistle: You have deeply wounded me.
Violet: I love you for your gentle charm and modesty.
Wintergreen: Be true until we meet again.

Cutting grass at the William D. Wood house in 1898. Then, as now, keeping the yard trim was generally a family affair. Not only that, but 'old dobbin' may have been the ultimate beneficiary enjoying fresh fodder in the hay mow. *Courtesy of the Seattle Historical Society*

Measures, Tables and Weights

Butter

1 lump the size of a medium egg equals 2 ounces.
1 tablespoonful of soft butter, well filled, equals 1 ounce.
4 heaping tablespoonfuls of soft butter equal 1 teacupful.
2 teacupfuls of packed soft butter equal 1 pound.
1 pint of well packed soft butter equals 1 pound.

Egg

8 large, or 10 medium sized, eggs equal 1 pound.

Cooking

One pound of soft butter is equal to a pint. Ten eggs are equal to a pound. A pound of brown or white sugar, powdered or loaf sugar, broken, equals a pint. A pound and two ounces of either wheat flour or corn meal is equal to a quart. Eight large tablespoonfuls are equal to a gill. Thirty-two large tablespoonfuls equal a pint. A common sized wineglass holds four tablespoonfuls, or half a gill. A common sized tumbler holds half a pint or sixteen large tablespoonfuls. Four ordinary teacups of liquid equal a quart.

Cooking

1	cup equals	½ pint or regular measuring cup
4	tablespoonfuls	¼ pint or regular measuring cup
1	gill equals	½ pint or regular measuring cup
1	pint equals	1 pound
1	cup of butter	½ pound
2¼	cups powdered sugar	1 pound
2	cups of sifted flour	½ pound
	1 rounding tablespoonful of flour	½ ounce
1	rounding tablespoonful of sugar	1 ounce
1	rounding tablespoonful of butter	1 ounce

Flour

2 heaping teaspoonfuls equal 1 heaping tablespoonful.
2 heaping tablespoonfuls equal 1 ounce.
5 heaping tablespoonfuls equal 1 teacupful.
5 teacupfuls of sifted flour equal 1 pound.
3½ level teacupfuls of corn meal equal 1 quart.
1 quart of sifted flour equals 1 pound.

Table for Blanching

The following table shows blanching time for vegetables:

Beets	2 minutes
Cabbage	3 to 4 minutes
Carrots	2 minutes
Cauliflower	4 to 6 minutes
Celery	2 to 3 minutes
Garden peas	3 to 5 minutes
Green string beans	5 to 8 minutes
Lima beans	3 minutes
Okra	3 minutes
Parsnips	2 minutes
Potatoes	2 to 3 minutes
Pumpkin and Winter squash	3 to 6 minutes
Spinach	2 minutes
Summer squash	3 to 6 minutes
Sweet corn	8 to 12 minutes
Sweet potatoes	6 to 8 minutes
Tomatoes	1 to 2 minutes
Wax beans	3 minutes

Table of Syrups for Canning

One pint sugar and 1 gill of water gives sirup of 40° density: Use for preserved strawberries and cherries.

One pint sugar and one-half pint water gives sirup of 32° density.

One pint sugar and 3 gills water gives sirup of 28° density: Use either this or the preceding for preserved peaches, plums, quinces, currants, etc.

One pint sugar and 1 pint water gives sirup of 24° density: Use for canned acid fruits.

One pint sugar and 1½ pints water gives sirup of 17° density.

One pint sugar and 2 pints water gives sirup of 14° density: Use either of these two light sirups for canned pears, peaches, sweet plums, and cherries, raspberries, blueberries, and blackberries.

The Number of Bushels in a Bin

Multiply together the three dimensions in feet to get the number of cubic feet and deduct 1/5 and you will have approximately the number of bushels in the bin.

Number of Gallons in a Barrel or Cask

Add the greatest and the smallest diameters in inches together and divide by 2 and this will be the average diameter. Multiply this number by itself, then by the length of the barrel in inches and then by 34 and cut off the four right-hand figures. This is approximately the number of gallons. Example—A cask is 28 inches in diameter at the head and 32 inches at the bung and is 36 inches in length; 28 plus 32 equals 60, divided by 2 equals 30, or the average diameter; 30 times 30 equals 900; 36 times 900 equals 32400; 34 times 32400 equals 1101600 and cutting off the four right-hand figures leaves 110 as the number of gallons.

Hay Measure

Fifteen to eighteen cubic yards of hay well settled in mows or stacks make a ton; 20 to 25 cubic yards make a ton when loaded on a wagon from mow or stack; 25 cubic yards of dry clover make a ton. To find the number of tons in a mow multiply the length, width and height in yards and divide by 15 if well settled and by 18 if not so well settled.

Miscellaneous Weights

100 lbs. nails	equal 1 keg
196 lbs. flour	equal 1 barrel
200 lbs. beef or pork	equal 1 barrel
280 lbs. N. Y. salt	equal 1 barrel

Omens

When found in the evening, a spider signifies good luck.

Daddy-long-legs are always messengers of good luck.

If your shoe or apron string breaks, your sweetheart is thinking of you.

If your right ear tingles, some one is speaking well of you; the left ear, some one is speaking ill of you.

To drop a dishcloth, duster, or any cleaning cloth, signifies the arrival of one or more visitors.

If a vacant rocking-chair is rocked violently, the next person who sits in it will be in danger of being ill within a year.

It is a lucky sign to have crickets in the house.

The right hand itching is a sign that the person will shake hands with a stranger; the left hand itching is a sign that money will be received anon.

To find a four-leaved clover brings good luck.

To drop a slice of bread with the buttered side down is a sign that a visitor will come hungry.

It is unlucky to present a knife, scissors, razor, or any sharp instrument to one's mistress or friend as it is apt to destroy the love and friendship. To avoid this a pin, penny or some trifle must be received in return.

To see a new moon, over the left shoulder is a sign of bad luck. To see a new moon over the right shoulder is good luck.

Weather Omens

Red clouds in the sunset mean the next day will be fair.

If spiders work at their webs early in the morning there will be a fine day.

If it rains before sunrise, the afternoon will be fine.

If there is a rainbow during the continued wet weather, the storm is passing.

If a leech is kept in a glass jar about three parts full of water and is placed in a northern aspect, its motions will foretell weather changes. If the leech is curled up at the bottom of the jar, the weather will be fine or frosty. If it is agitated and rises to the surface of the water there will be rain, wind or snow. If it be greatly agitated and creeps entirely out of the water, you can expect thunder. Leeches often die in great numbers during heavy storms.

If at sunrise many dark clouds are seen in the west, there will be rain on that day.

If the sunset is pale or purple there will be rain or wind the following day.

If the full moon rise pale it will be wet. If the full moon rise red, there will be wind.

If small, white clouds with rough edges are gathering there will be wind.

A rainbow in the morning is the shepherd's warning.

If old and rheumatic persons complain of their corns and joints and limbs once broken ache, the weather will be foul and wet.

It will rain if the marigold remains shut after seven in the evening.

If sheep and goats spring about in the meadow there will be bad weather; or if asses shake their ears, bray and rub against walls or trees; if cattle leave off feeding and chase each other in their pastures; if cats lick there bodies and wash their faces; if swine be restless and grunt loudly; if horses stretch their necks and sniff the air and assemble in the corner of a field.

The weather will be bad if the cock crows more than usual; if swallows fly lower than usual, if fish bite more readily; if worms creep out of the ground; if frogs and toads croak more than usual, if the owl screech.

If the fire burns fierce and bright in the winter there will be frost and clear weather; if the fire burns dull, expect damp and rain.

Water Witching

Not everyone can witch water. Education, sensitivity, race or measure of intelligence does not seem to affect the ability of a person to witch water. One with this ability is a valuable asset to a community, soon becomes known far and wide and is in great demand by those trying to locate sites for wells.

To witch water, you will need a divining rod or water witching wand. The rod or wand is made by selecting a forked branch of a tree. Some diviners prefer willow and others peach. The branches should be large enough to grasp with the hands and can be from twelve to eighteen inches in length. Leave enough of the limb or branch from the point where it separates into branches to the end to make a good pointer, at least six to eight inches in length.

To locate water, grasp one of the forks in each hand and hold firmly but not too tightly. Extend the point out in front of you and walk back and forth across the area which has been selected for a well. If there is water underground you will feel a tug or pull and the wand will dip and point to the ground without any exertion on your part. You will improve with practice and will find the wand will point down with such force that it will be difficult to keep it in an upright position. If water is not located at the site preferred, walk in an ever enlarging circle or make a criss-cross pattern covering the surrounding area.

An experienced water witch can tell the depth of the water source by dipping. To dip a well, hold the wand out over the place where you have located the water. The wand or rod will dip. Counting one dip for each foot of depth you can accurately predict the depth at which water will be found.

A good water witch is much sought after and the skill will provide a good living as barter for food or trade for services.

Bringing in the sheaves by ox team. Ox teams were used more extensively than horses or mules by the early pioneers. Oxen had a higher rate of survival in making the long journey because they could eat native forage along the way upon which horses could not survive. The men and women planning to make the trip by wagon train were advised not to plan on buying oxen and cows upon their arrival. Scarcity of good stock created exorbitant prices. *Courtesy of the Seattle Historical Society*

ACKNOWLEDGEMENTS

Abraham, Terry, *Washington State University Library*
Burke, Mrs. James T.
Connette, Dr. Earle, *Washington State University Library*
Crosby, Jim
Ellensburg Public Library, *Rare Books Department*
Ferris, Mr. and Mrs. Marlin
Griswold, Porter
Hilton, Mrs. Alice
Merritt, Mrs. Fern
Moeur, Mrs. Michael K.
National Archives, Washington, D.C.
Nolan, Edward, *Seattle Historical Society Library*
Paul, Mrs. Jean E.
Schnebly, Mr. and Mrs. Dorse A.
Shelton, Miss Frances
Taylor, Mrs. Edith
United States Department of Agriculture, *Farm Bulletins*

THE AMERICA

Is the BEST REFRIGERATOR MADE, and has the following superior points:

- Pure dry air.
- Perfect circulation.
- Patented removable galvanized steel ice compartment.
- Most economical in ice consumption.
- Absence of odors.
- Freedom from moisture on walls.
- Direct drainage to drip pipe.
- Divided shelf.
- Swinging fall board.

Order a sample to compare with the one you are now handling and be your own judge, or send for catalogue.
OUR PRICES ARE RIGHT.

H. GRUENHAGEN,
Northwestern Agent,
ANTHONY PARK, MINN.

The Bowen Manufacturing Co.,
Fond du Lac, Wis

MEN and WOMEN

Who have suffered years from lingering and wasting diseases **CAN BE CURED** quickly, safely, **and permanently**

By the great Electrical and Medical Specialists of this Institute.

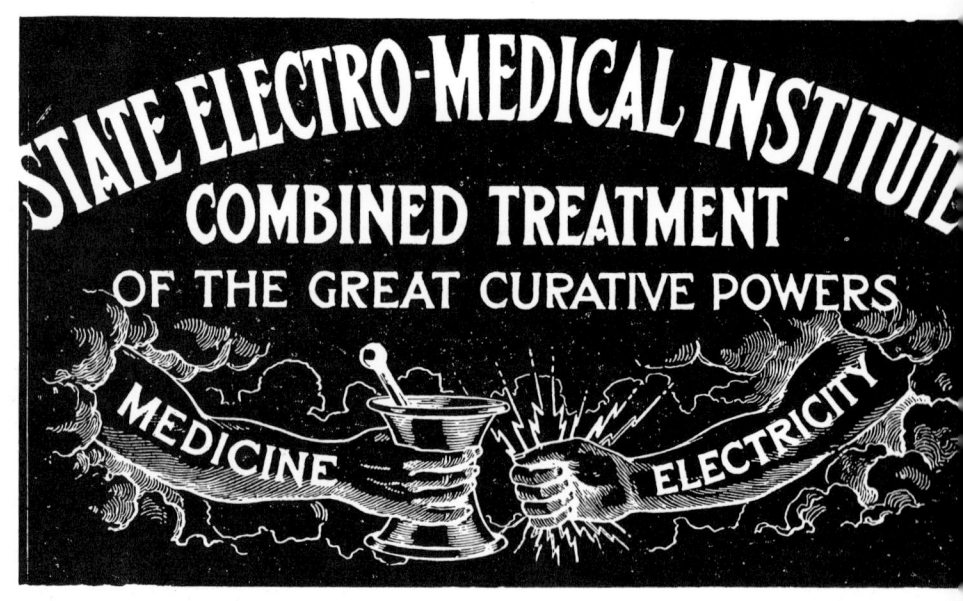

These specialists are among the best, most successful and scientific the world has ever known, and are achieving results in curing the sick and suffering by their Electro-Medical treatment which would be impossible to secure by either electrical or medical treatment alone. The State Electro-Medical Institute is the **ONLY PLACE** where you can obtain the benefits of this successful treatment under the most skilful and learned specialists. BE ASSURED that if any power on earth can cure you these doctors can—

—WHEN ALL OTHERS FAIL—

Remember the wonderfully successful specialists and treatment of this institute combine the two greatest factors of the healing art known to the medical profession—**ELECTRICITY and MEDICINE**. It is the largest, most thoroughly and completely equipped institute, both electrically and medically, ever established in the Northwest for the treatment and absolute cure of all nervous, chronic and private diseases of **Men and Women**. Honorable and fair dealing accorded to all.

WRITE IF YOU CANNOT CALL. All correspondence in plain envelopes. Confidential.

ADDRESS:

STATE ELECTRO-MEDICAL INSTITUTE,
301 Hennepin Avenue, Corner Third Street, MINNEAPOLIS, MINN.

ARRIVES

Detroit 8:10 p. m. same day.
Niagara Falls 4:2- a. m. next day.
Buffalo 5:00 a. m. next day.
New York 3:30 p. m. next day.
Boston 7:00 p. m. next day.

The only line running **FREE RECLINING CHAIR CARS** Chicago to Niagara Falls, Buffalo and New York without change. Leaving Chicago 3:15 p. m. and 11:30 p. m. daily for Detroit, Toronto, Montreal, Buffalo, New York and Boston.

TICKET OFFICE:
97 Adams St., Chicago, Ill.

F. A. PALMER,
A. G. P. A., Chicago, Ill.

or

G. J. LOVELL,
N. W. P. A., St. Paul, Minn.

"Let the GOLD DUST TWINS do your work"

Get the Original

Washing Powders of various makes are as thick as blackberries in August, but

GOLD DUST

is the only one that stands out above the heads of all others. It is the World's Greatest Cleanser.

No borax, ammonia, naptha, or other foreign ingredient is needed with GOLD DUST. It will do all the work without other assistance.

| GOLD DUST GENERAL USES FOR | Washing clothes and dishes, scrubbing floors, cleaning wood work, oil cloth, silverware and tinware, polishing brass work, cleaning bath room, pipes, etc., softening hard water and making the finest soft soap. |

We do Half your Washing Free of Cost

YOU must pay the washer-woman fifteen cents an hour.

It is hard-earned money at that. If you do your own washing, or have the servant do it, this steaming, back-breaking, hand-chapping, cold-catching, temper-destroying work will cost you more than 15 cents an hour, in the end.

It takes eight hours hard labor to do the average family wash.

Eight hours, at 15 cents, cost you $1.20 per week for washing.

This means $62.40 per year, without reckoning fuel for fires, or wear on clothes.

We will save you half of that—or No Pay.

We will send any reliable person our "1900" Washing Machine on a full month's free trial.

It runs on ball-bearings like a bicycle, and it works with motor-springs.

These motor-springs do most of the hard work.

You can sit in a rocking chair and make them do the washing—think of that!

We don't want a cent of your money, nor a note, nor a contract, when we ship you the Washer on trial. We even pay all of the freight out of our own pockets, so that you may test the machine as much as you like before you agree to buy it.

Use it a full month at our expense. If you don't find it does better washing, in half the time—send it back to the railway station, with our address on it—that's all.

We will then pay the freight back, too, without a murmur.

But, if the month's test convinces you that our "1900" Washer actually does 8 hours washing in 4 hours time—does it twice as easy—far better, without wearing the clothes, breaking a button, or tearing a thread of lace, then you must write and tell us so.

* * * *

From that time on you must pay us, every week, part of what our machine saves you, say 50 cents per week till the Washer is paid for.

Each "1900" Washer lasts at least five years, yet a very few months, at 50 cents a week, makes it entirely your own, out of what it saves you on each washing.

Every year our Washer will save you about $31.20 that you would have had to spend for labor of your own, or the labor of others.

In five years each machine saves its owner about $156.00. Yet the "1900" Washer won't cost you a cent, under our plan, because we let it pay for itself. You need not take our word for that. We let you prove all we say, at our expense, before you decide to buy it on these terms.

Could we risk the freight both ways, with thousands of people, if we did not know our "1900" Washer would do all we claim for it?

It costs you only the two-cent stamp, on a letter to us, to bring this quick and easy Washer to your door, on a month's trial.

That month's free use of it will save you about $2.00. You thus risk nothing but the postage stamp to prove our claims, and we practically pay you $2.00 to try it.

This offer may be withdrawn at any time if it crowds our factory.

Therefore WRITE TODAY, while the offer is open, and while you think of it. A post card will do.

Address me personally for this offer, viz:

R. F. Bieber, General Manager of the "1900" Washer Company, 917 North Henry Street, Binghamton, N. Y., or 355 Yonge Street, Toronto, Canada.

Catalogues Free to All.

Gentlemen: Sometime ago I purchased one of your "Full Swing Buggies with Rubber Tire," and I must say, so far, it has given me entire satisfaction. It looks well and is very comfortable to ride in. It is undoubtedly the best buggy I ever bought for the price.
Yours respectfully,
OLOF SOHLBERG, M. D.
East Seventh Street.
Dated, St Paul, Minn., Jan. 13, '99.

Gentlemen: The "Full Swing Rubber Tire Buggy" bought of you in the spring of 1898 has given very good satisfaction and a good deal of comfort. I have given it very rough wear. It is a delight to ride in it. You are entitled to great success with this vehicle. In driving through the streets of the city, I have noticed a great many of your vehicles among the members of my profession. Yours very truly,
E. A. BORCHARDT, M. D.
Dated, St. Paul, Minn., Jan. 4, '99.

We are Manufacturers.

Notice at the Hub, between the Twin Cities, is located the Minnesota Transfer, with ten railroads and MUCKLE'S GREAT VEHICLE PLANT, all on the Interurban Electric Street Car Line

No. 656 "NEW ERA," Light Surry.

For Mother and the Children.

H. A. Muckle Mfg. Co.,
ST. PAUL, MINN.

With or Without Rubber Tires.

Gentlemen: The "Full Swing Buggy" I purchased of you last summer has given me perfect satisfaction. It is one of the best buggies I ever rode in. For rough roads it has no equal. I can say that whoever buys a "Full Swing Buggy" will be pleased with it. I shall always be glad to recommend your firm to any one wishing to buy a buggy.
Yours very truly,
HENRY LENHARD.
Dated, Darwin, Minn., Jan. 23, '99.

Gentlemen: Last June I purchased one of your "Full Swing Open Buggies," and during the summer gave it some very severe tests over rough country roads. It beats any and all of them for comfort, ease and durability. We advise any one thinking of purchasing a vehicle, and who wishes to avoid sudden jerks by horse starting, or jolts on rough roads, to get a "Full Swing" by all means. Yours very truly,
J. C. PENNIMAN, Minneapolis Fire Dept. Minneapolis, Minn., Jan. 1, '99.

121

UTOPIA YARN

The Yarn of Quality
The Yarn that always gives Satisfaction

Because
- of its high standard of excellence
- of its perfect spinning
- of its superior dye and uniform shadings
- of its absolute reliability
- it is the <u>best</u> yarn that human ingenuity can produce

The Utopia Yarn Book is the most complete and practical Yarn book ever published. It covers the entire subject of knitting and crocheting thoroughly and contains absolutely reliable instructions for the making of all articles.

Price, 25 Cents

At all dealers of Utopia Yarn, or send stamps to the

Manufacturers of Utopia Yarns

457 Broome Street
New York

INDEX

Almond dust, 51
Almond paste, 51
Animal fats, 6
Apple butter with cider, 72
Apple butter with grape juice, 72
Apple Dicky, 51
Apple dumplings, 51
Apple jelly, 67
Apple or fruit cups, 51
Apples, how to dry, 80
Apple pancakes, 38
Apple vinegar, 84
Apricots, how to dry, 80
Arbor Vitae, remedy, 80
Atrificial goat's milk, 45
Ashes/vinegar, remedy, 86
Asparagus, remedy, 86
Aspic jelly, beef, 14
Aspic, vegetable, 62
Axle grease, how to make, 104

Bachelor's Buttons, 51
Baked Lake Trout, 25
Baked or boiled carrot pudding, 54
Baking powder, 35, 36
Baking soda, remedy, 86
Barbecued beef, 11
Barberry, remedy
Barley water, 38
Barometer, to make, 104
Barrel or cask, to measure, 114
Basic Diet, 6
Bayberry, remedy, 87
Beaten biscuits, 36
Beef brisket/sauerkraut, 13
Beef dried, fricasseed, 14
Beef jerky, 14
Beef juice, 15
Beef recipes, see Meats
Beer yeast, 34
Bees wax, remedy, 87
Beetroot, 59
Beets, how to dry, 79
Beets, remedy, 87
Berries, when dried, 81
Beverages
  Beers, 42
    Cottage, 42
    Ginger, 42
    Hop, 42
    Spruce, 42
  Drinks, 41, 42
    Coffee, 41
    Elder flower water, 41
    Farmers' soda, 41
    Grape wine, unfermented, 41
    Kentucky egg nog, 41
    Oatmeal drink, 41
    Peppermint cordial, 42
  Teas
    Beef, 17, 19
    Camomile, 42
    Linseed, 42
  Wines
    Blackberry wine, 42

Dandelion, 44
Elderberry, 43
Elder Blossom, 43
Honey, 44
Orange, 44
Blackberry jelly, 68
Blackberry, remedy, 87
Blackberry wine, 42
Black-Currant jelly, 68
Black-Currant vinegar, 84
Blanching vegetables, 78
Blue Violet, remedy, 87
Boiled beef dinner, 11
Boiled beef neck, 11
Boiled cider, 75
Boiled ham, 20
Bone soup, 31
Bone stock, 24
Boots, to blacken, 107
Boots, to dry, 107
Boracic acid, remedy
Borax and camphor, remedy
Boston baked beans, 58
Bottles, to clean, 100
Bouillon, 12
Boxwood, remedy, 87
Bran, remedy, 87
Bran tea/soup, 39
Breads and cereal foods
  Breads, how to bake, 34
  Bread, salt raising, 34
  Bread, starters, 34
    Beer, 34
    Hop, 34
    Potato, 34
    Yeast, cakes, 35
    Yeast, dried, 35
Breads, quick
  Baking powder, 36
  Beaten biscuits, 36
  Corn bread, 37
  Corn pone, 37
  Gingerbread, 37
  Gingerbread, soft, 37
  Indian fried bread, 37
  Self-raising flour, 36
  Shepherder's Dough Gods, 37
  Spoon bread, 37, 40
  Squaw bread, 37
Cakes, fried
  Apple pancakes, 38
  Hush Puppies, 38
Cereal foods
  Barley water, 38
  Cooked grain, 40
  Gonoquis, 39
  Gruel, 40
  Noodles, 38
  Porridge, hominy, 40
  Porridge, oatmeal, 40
Breath, to make pleasant, 104
Broth, lamb, 12
Broth, mutton, 12, 22, 24
Broth, sheep's head, 22
Broth, vegetable, 62
Brown Betty, 50
Brown Ragout, 11

Brown Steak, 12
Bushels, to measure, 114
Butter, to clarify, 45
Butter, to cut, 100
Butter, to freshen, 45
Butter, to keep firm, 100
Butter, to measure, 113
Butter, to store, 45
Butter, to substitute, 45

Cabbage, how to dry, 79
Cabbage, how to keep, 58
Cabbage, remedy, 87
Cakes, see Sweets
Cake, to level, 100
Camomile tea, 42
Campfire meal, 13
Camphor, remedy, 87
Candied fruit, 48
Candles, to save, 104
Candles, to shape, 104
Candy, see Sweets
Candy, cough drops, 50
Candy, how to make, 48
Canning, reminder, 100
Canning, syrups, 113
Caraway, remedy, 89
Carrots, how to dry, 79
Carrots, remedy, 89
Caustics, caution, 8
Cayenne, remedy, 88
Cayenne Pepper, etc., remedy, 88
Celery, how to dry, 79
Celery, remedy, 88
Cerates, 85
Chamomile, 89
Chammomilla tea, remedy, 89
Cheese, cottage, 45
Cheese, curd, 45
Cheese, Dutch, 45
Cherries, how to dry, 80
Cherries, preserved with currant juice, 70
Cherry preserves, 69
Chewing taffy, 49
Chili Con Carne, 13
Chili Sauce, 82
Chow Chow, 82
Christmas cakes, 50
Cider apple jelly, 68
Cider apple sauce, 75
Cider pear sauce, 75
Cinnamon drops, 49
Cinnamon Oil, remedy, 88
Clarified butter, 45
Clay, remedy, 88
Clear apples, 75
Clothing, to render uninflammable, 106
Coal, to save, 107
Coffee, 41
Coffee kringles, 51
Cold cream, 110
Cold tomato relish, 83
Cologne, 108
Colouring for fancy jellies, creams, etc., 48

123

Comfrey, remedy, 88
Consomme, 12
Cooked grain, 40
Cooking measures, 113
Compote of mixed fruits, 72
Corkscrew, to make, 104
Corn, 6
Corn bread, 37
Corn-flour, prevent salt hardening, 100
Corn meal poultice, remedy, 88
Corn pone, 37
Corn pudding, 53
Corn relish, 83
Cottage beer, 42
Cottage cheese, 45
Cottage pudding, 54
Covering jellies, 66
Crab-apple jelly, 68
Cracker custard, 53
Cracker Jack, 49
Cracknels, 24
Cranberries, how to keep, 77
Cranberry, remedy, 89
Cream, remedy, 89
Cress and dandelion salad, 62
Cress salad, 62
Cretonne, to wash, 100
Crops and vegetables, when to plant, 108
Croutons for soup, 32
Crunchy corn fritters, 60
Crusty beef roll, 13
Cucumber pickles, 83
Curd cheese, 45
Curing hams, 20
Currant jelly, 68
Curried fish, 25
Custard, see Sweets

Dahlia hoops, 64
Dandelion dish, 58
Dandelion greens, 58
Dandelion, remedy, 89
Dandelion wine, 44
Date pudding, 53
Decoctions, 85
Devilled ham, 20
Dewberry, remedy, 87
Dill pickles, 83, 84
Dough Nuts, 52
Dried beef, 14
Dried peach butter, 71
Dried yeast, 37
Drippings, to clarify, 24
Drying foods, 7
Drying fruits, method
  Apples and pears, 80
  Apricots, 80
  Berries, 81
  Cherries, 80
  Figs, 80
  Peaches, 80
  Plums, 80
  Prunes, 80
Drying vegetables, method
  Beets, carrots, parsnips, 79
  Cabbage, 79
  Lima Beans, 79
  Shell beans and peas, 79
  Sweet corn, 79
Duck, 27
Dutch cheese, 45

Egg Plant, 59
Eggs, 46
Elder Blossom wine, 43
Elderberry pie, 54
Elder Flower Tea and Cologne, 89
Elder-flower water, 41
Elderberry wine, 43
Empanadas with vanilla sauce, 55
Escalloped corn, 58
Extracts, 85

Fannie Farmer's Pudding, 54
Farmer's Soda, 41
Fat, to fry with, 100
Feathers, to curl, 107
Feathers, to fluff, 107
Fermentation and salting vegetables
  Green beans, 81
  Sour-crout, 81
Figs, how to dry, 80
Fish, 24, 25
Fish balls, 24
Flavouring spices, 33
Flaxseed, remedy, 89, 90
Flaxseed tea, remedy, 90
Flies, to rid of, 103
Flour, to measure, 113
Flowers, the meaning of, 111
Fluid extracts, 85
Fomentations, 86
Food grains, 6
Forcemeat, egg, 46
French mustard, 33
Freshair, remedy, 90
Freshening butter, 45
Fried beets, 58
Fruit, botanical description, 64
Fruit, how to dry, 80
Fruits, preserved in grape juice, 75
Fruit, preserves, 69
Fruit pricker, 67
Fruit pureés, 75
Fruit syrups, 77
Fruit selecting for preserving, 65
Furniture, to polish, 100, 101

Game, 27
Garanches, 16
Garden peas, how to dry, 79
Garlic, remedy, 90
German Potato Pancakes, 61
Ginger beer, 42
Gingerbread, 37
Gingerbread snaps, 51
Ginger pears, 77
Ginger, remedy, 90
Ginseng, remedy, 90
Glass decanter, to clean, 101
Glass, to cut or break, 104
Glass, to temper, 104
Glue substitute, 103
Gold chains, to clean, 101
Golden Rod, remedy, 90
Gonoquis, 39
Goose, 27
Gooseberry conserves, 72
Gooseberry jam, 68
Grapes, how to keep, 77
Green beans, salted, fermented, 81
Green gooseberry jelly, 68
Green-grape jelly, 68
Green salad, 62
Green tomato pickle, 83
Gruel, 40

Haggis, 22
Hair pomade, 111
Hair stimulant, 111
Hamburg steak, 14
Hand creams, 110, 111
Hasenpfeffer, 28
Hay, to measure, 114
Head cheese, 20
Herbs, dried, how to, 85
Herbs, how to use, 85
Herbs, powdered, 85
Hinges, to prevent creak, 107
Hog's lard, remedy, 90
Hollyhock, remedy, 91
Home cement, to make, 104
Homestead Law, portion of, 9
Homestead Law, 6
Hominy Porridge, 40
Honey and vinegar, remedy, 91
Honey wine, 44
Hop beer, 42
Hops, remedy, 91
Hop tea, remedy, 91
Hop yeast, 34
Horehound candy, remedy, 91
Horseradish, etc., remedy, 91
Hough or Shin soup, 31
Household remedies, 7
Horseradish sauce, 33
Humble pudding, 54
Hush puppies, 38

Indian fried bread, 37
Indian pudding, 54
Indian turnips, remedy, 91
Infusions, 85
Invalid jelly, 22
Irish stew, 23

Jellied veal, 19
Jerusalem artichokes, 60
Johnny cake, 51

Kale or curly greens, 59
Kansas chili, 15
Kentucky egg nog, 41
Kidney pudding, 22

Labels, to stick, 104
Lamb and mutton, see Meats
Larder, to keep fresh, 100
Leeks, 59
Leek soup, 31
Lemon juice, prevent discoloring, 100

Lemon, remedy, 91
Lentil and rice soup, 31
Lentil cutlets, 60
Lentil soup, 31
Lettuce and cucumbers, remedy, 92
Lettuce, remedy, 91
Lima beans, how to dry, 79
Lincoln, Abraham, 6, 10
Liniments, 86, 108
Linoleum or oilcloth, how to clean, 101
Linseed tea,
Lotions, 111
Lycopodium, remedy, 92
Lye, to make, 110

Mail, to prevent from being read, 107
Marigold, remedy, 92
Marmalades, 92
Marzipan, 51
Mayonnaise, 46
Measures, cooking, 113
Measures, miscellaneous
Meats
  Beef
    Barbecue pit, 11
    Barbecue pit, 11
    Boiled dinner, 11
    Boiled neck, 11
    Brisket, 13
    Campfire meal, 13
    Chili Con Carne, 13
    Chili, Kansas, 15
    Crusty roll, 13
    Curing, 13
    Dried, 14
    Dried, fricasseed, 14
    Drippings, 24
    Garanches, 16
    Hamburg steak, 14
    Hash, Red Flannel, 17
    Jerky, 14
    Jelly, 14
    Juice, 15
    Mincemeat, 23, 24
    Pasties, 15
    Pemmican, 15
    Pickled, 15
    Pot roast, 15
    Potted, 15
    Pressed, 17
    Ragout, brown, 11
    Short ribs, 18
    Smoked, 17
    Spitted, 16
    Stew, 17
    Stew with dumplings, 17
    Stew, Wagoneer, 16
    Stock, bone, 24
    Stock or bouillon, 12
    Stock, quick-made, 13
    Suet, to clarify, 24
    Tacos, 16
    Tamalie pie, 18
    Tea, 17, 19
    Tongue, pickled, 17
  Calf and Veal
    Brains, 22

    Jelly, calf, 18
    Jellied veal, 19
    Jelly, invalid, 22
    Stock, white, 24
  Ham and Pork
    Boiled, 20
    Curing, 20
    Devilled, 20
    Cracknels, 24
  Pork
    Head cheese, 20
    Pickled, 15
    Scrapple, 21
    Smoked, 17
  Lamb and Mutton
    Broth, 12, 22
    Brains, 22
    Haggis, 22
    Jelly, invalid, 22
    Kidney pudding, 22
    Stew, Irish, 23
  Fish
    Fish balls, Norwegian, 24
    Curried, 25
    Salmon, kippered, 25
    Trout, 24, 25
    Whiting, 25
  Game
    Ducks, roasted, 27
    Game, roasted, 27
    Goose, roasted, 27
    Pigeon, pie, 27
    Rabbit, 28
    Rabbit, Hasenpfeffer, 28
    Rabbit, stew, 28
    Venison roast, 29
    Venison sauerbraten, 29
    Venison steak, 29
  Soups
    Bone, 31
    Hough or Shin, 31
    Leek, 31
    Lentil, 31
    Lentil, pea, barley, rice, 31
    Lentil and rice, 31
    Mulligatawny, 31
    Ox-tail, 31
    Poultry, 31
    Soup, croutons, 32
    Soup, thickening, 32

Metal or iron articles, to mend, 103
Mice, to rid of, 103
Milk and red pepper, remedy, 92
Milk, to keep, 100
Milkweed, remedy, 92
Mincemeat, 22, 24
Miscellaneous weights, 114
Mock Oyster soup, 61
Molasses taffy, 49
Moths, to rid of, 103
Musk, remedy, 92
Mustard lotion, remedy, 93
Mustard pickles, 84
Mustard plaster, remedy, 92
Mustard, remedy, 92
Mulligatawny, 31
Mutton suet, remedy, 92

Nasturtium seeds/capers, 33
Noodles, 38
Nut cutlets, 62
Nut loaf, 62
Nutmeg, etc., remedy, 93

Oatmeal drink, 41
Odor, to destroy, 104
Ointments, 85
Olive oil, remedy, 93
Omens, good, bad, 114
Omens, weather, 115
Onions, how to keep, 58
Onions, remedy, 93
Orange wine, 44
Oregon Grape or Salal jelly, 68
Ox-tail soup, 31

Parsley, how to keep, 58
Parsley, jelly, 69
Parsley, remedy, 93
Parsnips, how to dry, 79
Parsnips, how to keep, 57
Pasties, beef, 15
Peach butter, 72
Peaches, how to dry, 80
Peanut Brittle, 48, 49
Pears, how to dry, 80
Pectin, 65
Pemmican, 15
Peppermint cordial,
Peppermint, oil of, remedy, 95
Peppermint, remedy, 95
Peppermint or Spearmint tea, remedy, 95
Perfumed water, 110
Peroxide/vinegar, remedy, 93
Picililli, 82
Pickle, beef, ham, 15
Pickled flank, 15
Pickled onions, 84
Pickled vegetables and fruits
  Chili sauce, 82
  Chow Chow, 82
  Cold tomato relish, 83
  Corn relish, 83
  Cucumber pickles, 83
  Dill pickles, 84
  Green tomato pickle, 83
  Mustard Pickles, 84
  Onion pickles, 84
  Peaches, 82
  Pickilili, 82
  Spiced crab apples, 84
  Sweet pickled peaches, 84
  Table relish, 82
  Tomato catsup, 82
Pigeon pie, 27
Pioneer food, 6
Plain pastry, 55
Plants, how to gather and keep, 85
Plums, how to dry, 80
Plum jelly, 69
Population movement, 6
Pork cake, 51
Porridge, 40
Potato Birdies, 61

Potatoes and salt, remedy, 93
Potatoes, how to keep, 58
Potato skins, remedy, 93
Potato yeast, 34, 35
Pot roast,
Potted beef, 15
Potted meat, 24
Poultry, 6
Poultry soup, 31
Preparing vegetables for drying, 78
Preserves, jellies, jams, etc.
  Butters, how to make, 71
    Apple with cider, 72
    Apple with grape juice, 72
    Peach, fresh, 72
    Peach, dried, 72
    Texas plum, 72
  Compote with mixed fruits, 72
  Fruit preserved in grape juice, 75
  Jellies
    Apple, 67
    Blackberry, 68
    Black-currant, gooseberry, 68
    Crab apple, 68
    Green gooseberry, 68
    Grape, ripe, 68
    Oregon Grape or Salal berry, 68
    Parsley, 69
    Plum, 69
    Quince, 69
    Raspberry or currant, 69
    Red-currant, 69
    Rose hip, 69
    Strawberry, 69
  Preserves
    Cherry, 69
    Cherry-currant, 70
    Fruit, 69
    Plum, 70
    Quince, 71
    Strawberry, 71
    Rose hip, 71
    Tomato, 71
    White currant, 71
  Pureés, fruit, 75
Preserving eggs, 46
Pressed beef, 17
Prunes, how to dry, 80
Puddings, see Sweets
Pumpkin seed, remedy, 93

Quince jelly, 69
Quince preserves, 71
Quince seed, etc., remedy, 95

Rabbit, 28
Rabbit stew, 28
Raisin tea, remedy, 95
Raisins, to stone, 100
Raspberry and currant jelly, 69
Raspberry jelly, 69
Raspberry vinegar, 84
Ratafia icing, 51
Rats, to rid of, 103
Red ants, to rid of, 103
Red clover, remedy, 95
Red-currant jelly, 69
Red Flannel Hash, 17

Red flannel, to wash, 101
Red raspberry, remedy, 87
Remedies, herbs, plants, roots, gathering and use, 85
  Arbor Vitae, 86
  Ashes/vinegar, 86
  Asparagus, 86
  Baking soda, 86
  Barberry, 87
  Bayberry, 87
  Bearberry, 87
  Bees wax, 87
  Blackberry, red-raspberry, dewberry, 87
  Blue violet, 87
  Boracic acid, 87
  Borax and camphor, 87
  Boxwood, 87
  Bran, 87
  Cabbage, 87
  Camphor, 87
  Carrots, 89
  Carroway, 89
  Catnip, 89
  Cayenne, 88
  Celery, 88
  Chamomile, 89
  Chestnut, 89
  Cinnamon oil, 88
  Clay, 88
  Cloves, 88
  Comfrey, 88
  Corn meal poultice, 88
  Cranberry, 89
  Cream, 89
  Dandelion, 89
  Elder flowers, 89
  Flaxseed, 89
  Freshair, 90
  Garlic, 90
  Ginger, 90
  Ginseng, 90
  Golden rod, 90
  Hog's lard, 90
  Holly hock, 91
  Honey/vinegar, 91
  Hops, 91
  Hop tea, 91
  Horehound, 91
  Horseradish, 91
  Indian Turnips, 91
  Lemon, 91
  Lettuce, 91
  Lettuce/cucumbers, 92
  Lycopodium, 92
  Marigold, 92
  Milk/red pepper, 92
  Milkweed, 92
  Musk, 92
  Mustard, 92
  Mutton suet, 92
  Mutton lotion, 93
  Nutmeg, etc., 93
  Olive oil, 93
  Onion, 93
  Parsley, 93
  Peroxide/vinegar, 93
  Potatoes/salt, 93

  Potatoes/skin, 93
  Pumpkin seed, 93
  Peppermint, 95
  Quince seed, 95
  Red clover, 95
  Rhubarb, 95
  Saffron, 95
  Sage, 95, 96
  Salt, 96
  Sarsaparilla, 96
  Sloe jam, 96
  Sassafras, 96
  Spearmint, 96
  Spices, 97
  Spinach, 97
  Strawberries, 97
  Sumach, 97
  Sunflower/seeds, 97
  Sweet clover, 98
  Thyme, 98
  Tomatoes, 98
  Treacle, 98
  Turnips, 98
  Watercress, 98
  Wild cherry, 98
  Wintergreen, 98
  Witch hazel, 98
  Wood charcoal, 98
Reminders
  Cooking/food
    Butter, 100
    Cake, 100
    Canning, 100
    Corn flour, 100
    Fat, 100
    Larder, 100
    Lemon juice, 100
    Milk, 100
    Stoning raisins, 100
  Cleaning/washing
    Bottles, 100
    Clothing, 100, 102
    Cretonne, 100
    Furniture, 100, 103
    Glass decanters, 101
    Gold chains, 101
    Linoleum, 101
    Oil cloth, 101
    Red flannel, 101
    Stoves, 103
    Wall paper, 103
    Windows, 103
  Mending
    China, 103
    Earthenware, 103
    Metal, 103
    Miscellaneous reminders, 104-7
  Pests, to rid of
    Ants, 103
    Flies, 103
    Mice, 103
    Moths, 103
    Rats, 103
Ripe grape jelly, 68
Rhubarb, remedy, 95
Roasted wild duck, 27
Roast game, 26
Roast goose, 27

126

Roast venison, 29
Rolled oat cookies, 52
Roots, how to gather and keep, 85
Rose hip jelly, 69
Rose hip preserves, 71

Saffron, remedy, 95
Sage, remedy, 95
Sage tea, etc., remedy, 95, 96
Salad dressing, 46
Salads, 62
Salmon, to kipper, 25
Salt, remedy, 95
Salsify, how to keep, 57
Salves and plasters, 108
San Diego Orange Marmalade, 72
Sarsaparilla, remedy, 96
Scarlet or pickled tongue, 17
Scones, 53
Scones, Scotch, 52
Scrapple, 21
Sealed well, how to make, 106
Self-raising flour, 36
Sheepherder's dough gods, 37
Sheepskin, to cure, 104
Shell beans and peas, how to dry, 79
Shoo-fly pie, 55
Short ribs, 18
Skin refresher, 110
Sloe jam, remedy, 96
Smoked meats, 17
Soap, to make, 110
Soap, to save, 106
Soft gingerbread, 37
Smoked meats, 17
Soups, 31, 32
Sour-crout, 81
Spearmint, remedy, 96
Spiced crab apples, 84
Spiced currants, 75
Spices, remedy, 97
Spitted meat, 16
Spoon bread, 37, 40
Spots, to remove, 103
Spruce beer, 42
Squaw bread, 37
Steamed pudding, 54
Stew, 17
Stewed lettuce, 62
Stew with bread dumplings, 17
Stock, lamb, 12
Stock, mutton, 12
Stock, quick-made, 13
Storing butter, 45
Stove polish, to make, 103
Strawberry jelly, 69
Suet, to clarify, 24
Sun drying, vegetables and fruits, 78
Sunflower seeds, etc., remedy, 97
Sweet clover ointment, remedy, 98
Sweet clover, remedy, 98
Sweet corn, how to dry, 79
Sweet oil, remedy, 87
Sweet pickled peaches, 84
Sweets
  Baked goods
    Apple or fruit cups, 51
    Apple dicky, 51

    Bachelor's buttons, 51
    Brown Betty, 50
    Coffee kringles, 51
    Gingerbread Snaps, 51
    Rolled oat cookies, 52
    Scones, 53
    Scotch scones, 52
  Cakes
    Christmas, 50
    Johnny, 51
    Pork, 52
  Candy, how to make, 48
    Coloring, 48
    Cough drops, 50
    Chewing taffy, 49
    Cinnamon drops, 49
    Cracker jack, 49
    Fruit, candied, 48
    Marzipan, 50
    Molasses taffy, 49
    Peanut brittle, 48, 49
  Custards and puddings
    Cracker custard, 53
    Corn pudding, 53
    Carrot pudding, 54
    Date pudding, 53
    Fannie Farmer's pudding, 54
    Humble pudding, 54
    Indian pudding, 54
    Steamed pudding, 54
    Tipsy pudding, 54
  Dough Nuts, 52
  Pastry and pie, 54-5
    Elderberry pie, 55
    Pastry, plain, 54
    Shoe-fly pie, 55
  Toppings
    Almond dust, 51
    Almond paste, 51
    Rotafia icing, 51
Syrup gauge, 67

Table for blanching vegetables, 113
Table for testing candy, 48
Table relish, 82
Tacos, 16
Tamale pie, 18
Tea, beef, 17, 19
Teas, herbal, 46, 85
Testing eggs, 46
Texas plum butter, 72
Thickening for soup, 32
Thyme, remedy, 98
Tight rings, how to remove, 107
Tinctures, 86
Tipsy pudding, 54
Toffee, 49
Tomato catsup, 82
Tomato preserves, 71
Tomato, remedy, 98
Toppings, 71
Treacle, rmedy, 98
Tripe, 23
Tripe, to clean, 23
Trout, 24
Turnip, how to keep, 58
Turnip, remedy, 87, 98

Unfermented grape wine, 41
Utensils, to cure, 104

Vegetables, drying, advantages of, 78
Vegetables, how to keep, prepare, 57
  Cabbages, to keep, 58
  Onions, to keep, 58
  Parsnips and salsify, to keep, 57
  Potatoes, to keep, 58
  Turnips, to keep, 58
  Vegetables, sundrying, see section on drying
Vegetable dishes
  Beans, Boston baked, 58
  Beans, Yankee Clipper, 58
  Beets, fried, 58
  Beetroot, 59
  Corn, escalloped, 58
  Corn fritters, 60
  Dandelion, 58
  Egg plant, 59
  Kale or curly greens, 59
  Leeks, 59
  Lentil cutlets, 60
  Jerusalem artichokes, 60
  Mock oyster soup, 61
  Potato, 60
  Sauer krout, baked, 60
  Spinach, 62
  Stewed lettuce, 62
  Vegetable aspic, 62
  Vegetable broth, 62
Vegetable Salads
  Cress, 62
  Dandelion, 62
  Green, 62
  Watercress, 62
Vegetables, table for blanching, 113
Venison, 29
Venison sauerbraten, 29
Venison steak, 29
Venison, to remove taint, 106
Vinegar, 84
Vitamin A, 7
Vitamin C, 7

Wagoneer stew, 16
Wall paper, to clean, 103
Water, to purify, 115
Water, witching to locate, 115
Watercress, 62
Watercress, remedy, 98
Weights and measures, 113, 114
Weights, miscellaneous, 114
White currant preserves, 71
White stock, 24
Whitewash, to make, 107
Whiting, fried, 25
Wild cherry Bark, remedy, 98
Wild cherry syrup, remedy, 98
Windows, to clean, 103
Wintergreen, remedy, 98
Witch hazel, remedy, 98
Wood charcoal, remedy, 98
Wood, to petrify, 104
Writing fluid, to make, 107

Yeast cakes, 31